Reducing Vulnerability

Reducing Vulnerability

Child Sexual Abuse, Harassment, and Abduction Prevention Curriculum for Grades K-6

Marjorie Fink, C.S.W.

L P Learning Publications, Inc.
Holmes Beach, Florida

ISBN 1-55691-124-6

Learning Publications, Inc.
5351 Gulf Drive
P.O. Box 1338
Holmes Beach, FL 34218-1338

Printing: 5 4 3 2 1   Year: 2 1 0 9 8

Printed in the United States of America

Contents

Author's Note

From training thousands of educators over the years, I have developed an enormous respect for classroom teachers as well as a heightened awareness of their huge responsibility to the intellectual development and the well-being of students.

When I am invited by school administrators to train their staff in the use of curriculum materials, I know when I leave, the teachers have to first find the time and energy to incorporate yet another program into their already filled working days. While prevention education does add an additional teaching burden, please know that by doing so you will be helping children to better use their abilities and possibly save lives.

A victimized, vulnerable child is a handicapped child — often unable to succeed, grow, or reach their potential. A confident and assertive child who feels entitled to respectful, humane treatment and knows how to protect him or herself has the greatest chance of benefiting from supportive academic and emotional efforts. All children deserve that chance. It is my hope that the following information and curriculum materials help you meet that challenge.

Introduction

The greatest share of keeping children safe belongs to those in the learning environment — the educators and adults working with children on a daily basis. Developed to help promote a safe school environment and reduce children's vulnerability both in and outside of school, this teaching guide is intended to help educators recognize signs of abuse, encourage children to share their concerns early before abuse progresses into a more serious encounter, and provide help and support when needed.

The curriculum materials are designed to encourage children to see themselves as unique, special, and worthy of good treatment, empowering them with the knowledge and skills to stop or avoid abuse and turn to trusted adults for help. Although dealing with serious and difficult problems, this curriculum is non-threatening, positive, and engaging in order that educators are comfortable presenting the material and for students to feel good about themselves as a result of their participation.

The outgrowth of many years' expertise and experience in developing prevention programs, this manual's scope is both a comprehensive compilation of resources for educators as well as curriculum materials for use in the classroom. What makes this educational resource unique is the thoroughness of its factual information and activities. It provides educators with a variety of options and choices for teaching skills development, and is easily adaptable to different learning styles, age groups, and needs of students. Teachers across the country who have been trained in the use of this curriculum's classroom activities have reported their students have had a consistent positive response to the activities, materials, and resources included.

Reducing Vulnerability was developed to meet state education mandates for teaching child sexual abuse and abduction prevention as well as Title IX federal guidelines for teaching sexual harassment prevention on the elementary school level.

How the Material Is Organized

The curriculum is organized in three units. Each unit contains the notes to presenters, teaching guidelines, and resource materials in Part A, and curriculum materials in Part B.

Unit 1: Child Sexual Abuse Prevention

Unit 2: Teasing, Bullying, and Sexual Harassment Prevention

Unit 3: Child Abduction Prevention

Each unit can stand alone as a prevention program or taught sequentially as a comprehensive prevention program.

When taught as a comprehensive prevention program, the curriculum has been developed so that the child sexual abuse prevention concepts in Unit 1 coordinate with the concepts of prevention taught in both Units 2 and 3. It is recommended that the child sexual abuse component be taught first since the harassment and abduction components build upon the child sexual abuse prevention concepts. All components teach that children are entitled to respectful, humane treatment at home, in school, and in the community, from their peers as well as adults. Each unit serves as a reinforcement of skills learned in the other components. Students are enabled to apply skills to their knowledge base and are provided with multiple opportunities to build upon these skills.

Each unit suggests how to introduce the topic and lists classroom activities. The classroom activities are specifically geared for different age groups and the grade levels are clearly specified. Some activities are appropriate for K-6. Other activities indicate they have been developed specifically for grades K-3 or 4-6. In those cases the same prevention concepts are taught using different age-appropriate materials.

What the Curriculum Emphasizes

Part A: Resource Information Provides Educators with a Knowledge Base

Important resource information is provided for each topic before the activities are introduced to enable administrators and teachers to develop a working knowledge base and understanding of the problem. The information can also be used for staff training and developing effective responses to handling disclosures.

Having a working knowledge of child sexual abuse, sexual harassment, and abduction enables educators to teach these sensitive topics with a level of comfort. Well-informed teachers foster a non-threatening and positive learning environment for students. When the teachers are well informed, the children who have already participated in the classroom activities said it was fun learning about being safe and feeling good about themselves now that they know how to handle different situations.

Part B: Curriculum Materials to Build Self-Protection Skills

When made to feel uncomfortable or unsafe by an adult, a stronger child, or group of children, the child needs courage and confidence to be assertive. Providing knowledge is not sufficient. To truly empower children with the confidence and knowledge skills to protect themselves, they need to practice in many different ways. In reviewing the activities you will notice there is purposeful repetition. Whenever possible an activity will be used to introduce information and reinforce what has already been taught. Activities in each section provide several different opportunities to reinforce the same prevention concepts through videos, role plays, games, and scenarios.

Activities in each of the three units of the curriculum reinforce the skills learned in the other parts. Consistent language is used throughout the curriculum and prevention concepts overlap. You will be able to say, "Remember when we learned about . . . asserting ourselves, or trusting your feelings, or that it's not your fault?" or "Remember when we learned the importance of getting help? Let's role play that again but this time the situation will be . . . ".

Read through the curriculum in its entirety before teaching any of the prevention programs covered. This is important even if you will only be teaching one of the areas of prevention at this time. By doing so you will gain an overall perspective on how the curriculum builds and reinforces skill development. It will also give you a broader knowledge base which will be helpful when teaching any of the aspects of child victimization prevention covered in this teaching guide.

Unit 1: Child Sexual Abuse Prevention

Part A: Resource Materials for Educators

Note to Presenters

Although child sexual abuse tends to be under-reported, reported cases in the U.S. reveal alarming statistics such as one in four females and one in seven males are sexually abused before 18 years of age. Reports also indicate that one-half of the victims are 12 and under, and in 90 percent of the cases the abuser is someone the child knows. In over 60 percent of reported cases the abuser is someone in the child's family — someone the child knows, trusts, and even loves.

Child sexual abuse includes any contact or interaction between a child and an adult caretaker in which the child is being used for sexual stimulation. It always involves the abuse of power. When someone is bigger, older, and has more authority, that person is able to abuse another person — in this case a child — only because he or she is in a position of power and control. Children are vulnerable to sexual abuse simply because they are children and uninformed. Children who participate in prevention programs are far better equipped to avoid or stop some forms of sexual abuse. They are able to recognize that forced and secret touching can happen and is never OK.

Because child sexual abuse occurs in all social, economic, ethnic, and racial groups, and because children are so vulnerable, it is critical to implement programs that address the protection of children in school settings. Since potential child victims are likely to be alone with the abuser, it is the responsibility of adults to help keep children safe and teach them how to develop and use their own resources to protect themselves.

Many states require public school districts to teach sexual abuse prevention skills in the elementary school grades and it is encouraged in the middle and upper grades. These efforts have resulted in an increased awareness of the problem in the educational community and a need for effective educational resources. The Unit 1 materials are intended to help educators meet this requirement by including resources for educators and curriculum materials for use in the classroom.

Review the educational resource materials (Part 1A) before you proceed to the curriculum materials. These materials provide educators with information that promotes staff awareness and an understanding of the problem. This is important preparation to effectively utilize the curriculum materials which follow. The curriculum materials (Part 1B) have been developed to empower students with the knowledge and skills to stop or avoid sexual abuse. Through interactive and age-appropriate materials children learn that touching is one important way to take care of their special selves. The activities teach students to practice saying no in different ways and in loud assertive voices anytime someone hurts them or makes them feel uncomfortable. The activities stress the importance of telling, that it's never a child's fault, and promote assertive skills in asking for help.

The materials in both the sexual harassment and abduction sections (Units 2 and 3) are based and build on the concepts of child sexual abuse prevention. It therefore strengthens the other programs to teach Unit 1 first. In addition, the other prevention programs to reinforce the concepts taught in this first part as well.

Teaching Guidelines

Administrators: Prior to implementing the child sexual abuse program

■ Inform parents that children will be participating in this prevention program, prior to its implementation. This can be accomplished by inviting parents to an informational program to review videos, receive an overview of the program, and ask questions.*

■ Many schools also choose to send a letter to parents explaining that the school's student population will be participating in a state-mandated program to help reduce children's vulnerability to sexual abuse. This letter should reassure parents that the program is presented in a positive manner. It is helpful to explain that child sexual abuse is a preventable problem and the informed, prepared child is far better equipped to prevent or stop some forms of sexual abuse than the child who is not aware that it can happen. Parents should be encouraged to call with any questions about the program or concerns regarding their child's participation.

■ Conduct staff training that includes information on child abuse and its prevention, mandated reporting, school procedures for handing disclosures, and training in the use of curriculum materials.

■ Those uncomfortable with the subject matter should not teach the curriculum materials. In such cases provide for an alternative presenter.

Teachers/Presenters: Prior to implementing the program

■ Read and review this unit for information on handling student disclosures, mandated reporting, indicators of child abuse and maltreatment, and recognizing the academic and emotional clues of child abuse in the classroom.

■ Review your school's procedures on handling disclosures of child abuse and neglect.

■ Alert the building principal if there are concerns about any student's participation in the program.

■ Inform support personnel of the teaching schedule for the child sexual abuse prevention program so they will be prepared in the event a child discloses and needs further assistance.

■ Stress the seriousness and the importance of the topic with the class and the expectation that students will be on their best behavior.

---

*A resource for parents in pamphlet form that can be handed out at parent education programs is Marjorie Fink, *Protecting Children from Sexual Abuse.* (For more information see Resources.)

During the presentation all teachers should

- Remain in the classroom (in the event that a support person is the presenter).
- Actively observe students and be prepared to offer support when indicated.
- Make sure all students have an opportunity to participate and, therefore, do not allow exceptional excuses.

Following the presentation all teachers should

- Reinforce to students the availability for help if needed.
- Share any concerns about student(s) resulting from the program with the building principal.
- Reinforce everyone's right to their own bodies and respectful treatment not only outside of school but in the classroom and school as well.

Guidelines for Handling Disclosures in the School Setting

The material in this curriculum is designed to encourage children to communicate their concerns to a trusted adult in school. Because the importance of telling and getting help is stressed in every section of this curriculum, disclosures may result. In addition, it is not uncommon for children to bring concerns about other types of victimization when learning about any of the presented areas of prevention. For example, when children learn about peer harassment or abduction prevention, presenters may hear child sexual abuse concerns from students as well. Therefore, it is helpful and important to review the following guidelines for handling student disclosures prior to teaching Units 1, 2, and 3. Refer to these guidelines throughout the school year. They include information about mandated reporting, indicators of child abuse and maltreatment, and recognizing the academic and emotional clues of child abuse in the classroom.

Develop Procedures for Reporting Disclosure of Child Abuse*

- Each school district should establish procedures for handling disclosures and reporting suspected incidents of child abuse and neglect. Annual training of all staff should include the review of policies and procedures, information about mandated reporting, and identifying the physical and emotional abuse indicators.

- A school official (building principal or his or her designee) should assume the responsibility for reporting suspected child abuse and neglect to the proper state authorities.

- All school personnel should be informed regarding their responsibility to report suspected cases of child abuse and neglect to the designated school official. In the event the school official fails to make the report to the proper authorities and the staff person initiating the report continues to suspect abuse, that person should make the report directly to the child protection agency.

- The school official may assign a designee (for example, a school social worker) to be responsible for filing the written report (if required) with the appropriate agency. This person also may be asked to make the oral report to the agency and serve as the liaison person.

*From Marjorie Fink, *Adolescent Sexual Assault and Harassment Prevention Curriculum* (Holmes Beach, Fla.: Learning Publications, 1995), 9-21.

- There should be a school liaison in each building to follow-up with the agency handling the investigation and oversee the case. This is a vital role because it can prevent a child from falling through the cracks.

- In the event a child protection worker needs to interview a child on school property, it is advised that a school official be present during the interview. In the event a child protection agency representative comes to the school requesting an interview with a child without prior notification, a school official should contact the agency to verify the need for the interview, as well as identify the worker and the child.

- Determine whether the parents should be notified in cases of suspected child abuse. It is recommended that in cases of incest and physical abuse, when students usually need protection from further abuse, that the agency inform the parents following the student's interview. This may protect the student and also may prevent retractions of disclosure.

- Efforts should be made to protect the student's confidentiality.

- A resource team — comprised of school professionals who have training and experience dealing with physical, mental, and sexual abuse cases — should be designated to handle concerns regarding the abuse of a student. The team members should be knowledgeable about community resources, referrals, and reporting. The school's building official, who is responsible for reporting cases of abuse, and the designated liaison should be a member of this team. Team members should be available to serve as a resource for other school personnel, to students who need assistance handling abuse concerns, to aid in assessing risk of further harm to a student, to help determine procedures for parental notification, to coordinate services for the student and family when indicated, to handle the aftermath of an incident by providing support for other students concerned about the event, to help promote prevention programs for students, and provide training for staff.

Prepare for Handling Disclosures

Familiarize yourself with the established school procedure for handling disclosures. You will need to know the following:

- What should you do when a disclosure is made involving mandated reporting?

- What should you do when a disclosure is made in cases other than those involving child abuse such as peer abuse?

- Is there a written procedure to follow?

- Is there a designated person in the school to whom you report suspected cases of child sexual abuse or victimization by another student or peer?

- Who will need to meet with the student when a disclosure is made?

- Who is responsible for reporting cases of child abuse to child protective services?

- Is there a policy regarding parental notification?

Mandated Reporting*

Educators' involvement in the reporting of child abuse and neglect is mandated and supported by federal regulations as well as state laws. Since each state has it's own reporting statutes for child abuse and neglect, a checklist of questions for state reporting will be included at the end of each subsection. These questions represent the areas where states differ in their statutes and will facilitate obtaining the specific information of your state.

How Child Abuse and Neglect Is Defined

The first step in any child protection system is to identify possible incidents of child abuse and neglect. To prevent and treat child abuse and neglect effectively, a common understanding of the definition is necessary. This is provided by the Child Abuse Prevention and Treatment Act of 1974 which defines child abuse and neglect as "the physical or mental injury, sexual abuse or exploitation, negligent treatment, or maltreatment:

- of a child under the age of 18, or except in the case of sexual abuse, the age specified by the child protection law of the state;
- by a person (including any employee of a residential facility or any staff person providing out-of-home care) who is responsible for the child's welfare;
- under circumstances which indicate that the child's health or welfare is harmed or threatened thereby . . .".

The act further defines sexual abuse as "the use, permission, or coercion of any child to engage in any sexually explicit conduct (or any simulation of such conduct) for the purpose of:

- producing any visual depiction of such conduct, or rape, molestation, prostitution, or
- incest with children."

Within any given state there are different definitions of maltreatment. For example, in several states the age cutoff is raised or eliminated for older children with special needs such as disabled children. Consult your state law to determine the definitions of child maltreatment and the reporting procedures.

Questions for State Reporting

- What is the maximum age that a sexually abused person is considered a child under the child protection laws of your state?
- Is there a different age cutoff for older children with special needs?

---

*Adapted from *A Coordinated Response to Child Abuse and Neglect: A Basic Manual* (U.S. Department of Health and Human Services, 1992).

Who Must Report

State reporting laws specify certain professionals, classes of individuals, or institutions required to report suspected cases of child abuse and neglect. These laws also indicate those individuals permitted but not required to report abuse. Most identify the following as required to report:

- medical professionals such as physicians, nurses, dentists, and medical examiners;
- mental health professionals such as psychologists, therapists, or counselors;
- educators such as teachers and administrators;
- social service providers such as social workers and social services personnel;
- child-care providers such as staff in day-care centers, preschools, and family day care: foster parents and residential/institutional care personnel;
- law enforcement personnel.

All States

- Allow anyone to report a suspected case of child abuse and neglect. These reports are now handled through the same process as mandated reports.
- Accept anonymous reports. (However, this is not encouraged because it can hamper the investigation.)

Some States

- Require a report from any person who has reason to believe that a child is a victim of child abuse and neglect.
- Limit the requirements of professionals to report only situations known to them in their professional or official capacity.
- Require professionals to report their suspicions to the head of their agency or institution, who is then responsible for making the report.
- Make both the head of the agency and the individual staff member responsible for reporting. If there is disagreement about the need for a report, the staff member is required to make the report if he or she still has reason to suspect child abuse.

Questions for State Reporting

- Is it mandated by law that suspected child abuse be reported by any person or that only certain professionals report suspected child abuse?
- Are professionals required to report only those suspected child abuse cases that they learn about in their roles as professionals?
- Is the administrative head responsible for making a report? Does this requirement extend to individual staff if the administrator fails to make a report?

Reporting Immunity

Reporting laws also contain provisions to protect reporters from civil lawsuits and criminal prosecution resulting from filing a report in good faith. The immunity is provided as long as the report is made in good faith. In order to initiate a report, an individual must suspect that a child has been maltreated. Determining whether child abuse or neglect is substantiated (that some credible evidence exists) is the responsibility of the state or provincial agency charged with that responsibility and the courts. As long as the reporter has a basis to suspect that maltreatment has occurred, it is assumed that the report has been made in good faith, and therefore the reporter is immune from criminal or civil liability.

Failure to Report

Most states and provinces have criminal penalties for failure to report child abuse. There is also the risk of civil lawsuit liability for failure to report by those persons designated as mandated reporters. Typically, failure of a mandated reporter to report is punishable by fines and/or jail terms of usually six months or less. Since reporting laws vary, professionals should obtain a copy of their state's or province's reporting statutes and study it carefully. Failure to report may be inadvertent and may occur because of the lack of understanding of how to report by mandated reporters.

The following frequently cited mistakes result in the failure to report:

- Each separate incident requires a new and separate report to the child protection agency. Frequently if the agency is already involved, mandated reporters may call the local agency to find out "what's happening" when they suspect additional abuse rather than file an additional report. Each time child abuse is suspected it should be reported. This is crucial to establishing a pattern of abuse and further extends the time of agency involvement.

- An individual staff member may defer to the judgment of his or her administrator who is reluctant to report even though the staff person suspects abuse. The staff member may not recognize that he or she is mandated to report directly to the child protection agency if the administrator decides not to make the report to the agency.

- A mandated reporter may be reluctant to report suspected abuse without substantiation. He or she does not understand that it is not his or her responsibility to investigate the abuse. The determination of abuse is the responsibility of the child protection agency.

Questions for State Reporting

- Are there criminal penalties for failure to report? What are they?
- Is there civil lawsuit liability for failure to report?

How to Report

Oral Reports. Most states require oral reporting of child abuse to be made immediately to designated child protection agencies. All states encourage oral reports to be made either to a statewide hotline number, if available, or by calling the local child protection agency.

When an oral report is made an intake worker will ask detailed questions. The information requested will be similar to what is required in the written report. Do not delay making an oral report even if you do not have the information requested. Under the laws of every state the child protective agencies must accept and investigate all properly made reports.

Reported suspicions are not required to be proven that a child has been abused or neglected. All that is needed is a reasonable basis for suspecting maltreatment. Because child protection agencies often look for a pattern of abuse, documented reasons for suspecting abuse are recommended. This should be done by maintaining a log of concerns and observations that you can easily refer to for both your oral and/or written report.

Written Reports. Many states require that a written report follow the oral report. Some require written reports from mandated reporters. In other areas, written reports are to be filed only upon request. The time frame for submission of a written report may vary from within 24 hours to seven days of the initial oral report. Most states have special reporting forms that may be obtained from the local child protective agency. Many states have laws that make the written reports admissible evidence in court. Keeping a copy of the written report facilitates discussions with child protective services staff on behalf of the child suspected of being abused.

Where to Report. Every state designates a specific agency to receive reports of child abuse and neglect. In some states these agencies have the exclusive responsibility for receiving reports. In other areas the reports may be made to either the child protection agency or law enforcement. Sometimes, the law requires that physical or sexual abuse of a child be reported to the police in addition to reports made to the child protective agency.

The nature of the relationship of an alleged perpetrator may affect where reports are made:

- All alleged cases of child maltreatment within the family are reportable to the child protection agency.

- Depending on the state, allegations of abuse or neglect by other caretakers, such as foster parents, day-care providers, teachers, or residential care providers, may fall outside the purview of local child protection agencies.

- Depending on the state, alleged child maltreatment by someone outside the family is investigated by the agency and law enforcement, or is solely under the jurisdiction of law enforcement.

Contents of the Report. Reporting laws specify the required information, generally including:

- the name, age, sex, ethnic background, permanent address, and current whereabouts of the child;
- identifying information and current location of child's parents and siblings;
- identifying information and relationships to other adults and children in the home;
- identifying information and current location about the person alleged to have caused the child's condition;
- the nature and extent of the child's injuries or condition and need for emergency action;
- available information about prior injury or maltreatment to the child or siblings; and
- a description and date(s) of incident(s) and reasons to suspect alleged abuse including direct evidence such as eye-witness accounts and suspected indicators of abuse.

Questions for State Reporting
- Are oral reports required? If so, to whom?
- Are there specific state guidelines for an oral report?
- Is it required that a written report follow an oral report? If so, from whom? (Mandated reporters? All reporters?)
- Is there a time limit for submission of the written report?
- Is there a special reporting form and, if so, where can it be obtained?
- Are written reports admissible evidence in court?

Handling the Child and Family

As a professional mandated to report suspected cases of sexual abuse, you will often be the first person in the child protective system to have contact with a sexually abused child and his or her family. Sexual abuse allegations frequently create emotional difficulties for professionals and cause trauma for the child.

Keep your mind open to the possibility that sexual abuse may be occurring in the family situation. Be aware of your own feelings. Because sexual abuse usually evokes intense feelings, it will require an effort to maintain objectivity. A calm and professional approach is necessary to help and protect the child victim. Remember that disclosure of sexual abuse may lead to severe reactions by family members and may result in harm to the child.

If the child victim or another person discloses sexual abuse:
- Speak with the child or other person alone, to obtain his or her account of the alleged sexual abuse. Every effort should be made to provide privacy for the child and family. It is advisable to keep the number of involved staff to a minimum, in order to facilitate interaction and ensure privacy.

- Tell the child, or other person that you have heard this before and you know other children who have been sexually abused. This may encourage the child, or other person, to disclose information to you. It may also help to reduce the child's sense of isolation.

- Conduct the interview calmly, in a manner that puts you and the child, or other person, at ease. Use terminology that the child mentions or understands. Emphasize to the child that the sexual abuse was not his or her fault.

- Refrain from making judgments about the information given to you and avoid projecting your feelings onto the child or other person. For example, do not say, "That must have hurt you," or "That made you mad, didn't it?"

Recognizing Child Abuse and Maltreatment*

It is important that educators be able to recognize the signs of physical abuse, child neglect, sexual abuse, and mental injury (also referred to as emotional/psychological abuse). Sensitive educators can pick up cues of possible maltreatment by observing children's behavior at school, observing physical signs, or during routine interviews with parents.

The following information is provided to aid in the recognition of abuse and neglect. It is important to note that the recognition of child maltreatment is based upon a cluster of indicators that form a picture of abuse rather than on the detection of one or two clues.

Child physical abuse is characterized by physical injury (for example, bruises and fractures) resulting from punching, beating, kicking, biting, burning, or otherwise harming a child. Although the injury is not an accident, the parent or caretaker may not have intended to hurt the child. The injury may have resulted from overdiscipline or physical punishment that is inappropriate to the child's age or condition. The injury may be the result of a single episode or repeated episodes and can range in severity from minor bruising to death.

Any injury resulting from physical punishment requiring medical treatment is considered outside the realm of normal disciplinary measures. A single bruise may be inflicted inadvertently; however, old and new bruises on several areas of the face or bruising an infant suggest abuse. In addition, any punishment that involves hitting with a closed fist or an instrument, kicking, inflicting burns, or throwing the child is considered child abuse regardless of the severity of the injury sustained.

Child neglect is characterized by failure to provide for the child's basic needs. Neglect can be physical, emotional, or educational.

---

*Adapted from *A Coordinated Response to Child Abuse and Neglect: A Basic Manual* (U.S. Department of Health and Human Services, 1992).

Physical neglect includes refusal of or delay in seeking health care, abandonment, inadequate supervision, and expulsion from home or refusing to allow a runaway to return home.

Educational neglect includes permission of chronic truancy, failure to enroll a child of mandatory school age, and inattention to a special educational need.

Emotional neglect includes such actions as chronic or extreme spouse abuse in the child's presence, permission of drug or alcohol use by the child, and refusal or failure to provide needed psychological care.

It is important to distinguish between neglect and a parent or caretaker's failure to provide the necessities of life because of poverty or cultural norms.

Sexual abuse includes a wide range of behavior: fondling a child's genitals, intercourse, rape, sodomy, exhibitionism, and commercial exploitation through prostitution or the production of pornographic materials. Most state laws distinguish between sexual abuse and sexual assault. To be considered sexual abuse, these acts have to be committed by a person responsible for the care of the child (for example, a parent, babysitter, day-care provider, or other person responsible for a child). Sexual assault is usually defined as a sexual act committed by a person who is not responsible for the care of the child.

Sexual abuse involves varying degrees of violence and emotional trauma. The most commonly reported cases involve incest (sexual abuse occurring among nuclear family members), which most often occurs between father or stepfather and daughter. However, mother/son, mother/daughter, and brother/sister incest also occurs. Sexual abuse may also be committed by other relatives such as aunts, uncles, grandfathers, grandmothers, and cousins.

Emotional abuse includes acts or omissions by the parents or other persons responsible for the child's care that have caused, or could cause, serious behavioral, cognitive, emotional, or mental disorders. In some cases of emotional abuse, the parents' actions alone, even without any evidence of harm to the child, are sufficient to warrant intervention by a child protection agency, for example, when the parents or caretakers use extreme or bizarre forms of punishment, such as torture or confinement in a dark closet. For less severe acts, such as habitual scapegoating, belittling, or rejection, demonstrable harm to the child is often required for intervention by a public agency.

Emotional abuse is the most difficult form of child maltreatment to identify. First, the effects of emotional maltreatment, such as lags in physical development, learning problems, and speech disorders, are often evident in children who have not experienced emotional maltreatment. Second, the effects of emotional maltreatment may only become evident in later developmental stages in the child's life. Third, the behaviors of emotionally abused and emotionally disturbed children are often similar.

There are guidelines to help distinguish between emotional disturbance and emotional abuse. The parents of an emotionally disturbed child generally recognize the existence of a problem, whereas the parents of an emotionally abused child often blame the child for the problems or ignore the existence of a problem. The parents of an emotionally disturbed child show concern about the child's welfare and actively seek help, whereas the parents of an emotionally abused child often refuse offers of help, and may appear punitive or unconcerned about the child's welfare.

Although any of the forms of child maltreatment may be found alone, they often occur in combination. And, emotional abuse is almost always present when other forms are identified.

Indicators of Sexual Abuse

The following physical and behavioral signs, while in no way conclusive, should alert mandated reporters to the possibility of sexual abuse or maltreatment. Since these signs are only indicators, the mandated reporter should collect as much information as necessary to report suspected sexual abuse.

Physical Indicators
- Bruises on buttocks, inner thighs, or genitals.
- Bleeding in external genitalia, vaginal, or anal areas.
- Swelling, pain, itching, or cuts in genital or anal areas.
- Genital discharge, stains or blood on underclothes, or torn underclothes.
- Difficulty in walking or sitting.
- Venereal disease in children less than 18 years old.
- Pregnancy in children less than 18 years of age.

Behavioral Indicators
- Any changes in behavior such as loss of appetite, nightmares, and inability to sleep.
- Regression to more infantile behavior like bedwetting and thumb-sucking.
- Withdrawal from usual activities.
- Poor peer relationships.
- Fear of a person or intense dislike at being left somewhere or with someone.
- Unusual sexual knowledge or behavior that is inappropriate for age and development.
- Difficulty in concentrating at school.
- Aggressive or disruptive behavior, delinquency, or running away.
- Unwillingness to change for physical education class or to shower in front of peers.
- Discloses sexual abuse by caretaker.

Recognizing Child Abuse and Neglect in the Classroom*

Each form of maltreatment (physical abuse, neglect, sexual abuse, and emotional maltreatment) can be found among school-aged children. Sensitive educators can pick up clues of possible maltreatment by observing children's behavior and physical signs at school or during routine interviews with parents.

General Indicators of Abuse and Neglect

There are indicators that — rather than signaling the presence of one particular type of abuse or neglect — might serve as general signs that the child is experiencing abuse and/or neglect at home. These general indicators include academic clues and emotional/psychological clues.

Academic Clues

Academic performance can be a clue to the presence of child abuse and neglect. This is particularly true when there are sudden changes in performance. Previously good students who suddenly seem disinterested in school or who are no longer prepared for class may be emotionally maltreated. Athletes who suddenly refuse to change for gym class may be concealing evidence of beatings. Children whose broken glasses have not been replaced may no longer have someone looking after them.

Recent studies have revealed a relationship between child abuse and neglect and certain learning problems. For example, Cornell University's Family Life Development Center matched maltreated children with 530 children who had not suffered abuse or neglect. They evaluated the school performance of each child based upon grades, grade repetition, achievement test scores, and other school adjustment issues such as truancies, suspensions, and infractions of disciplinary codes. Distinctions were also made between 120 maltreated children who had been treated by local service agencies and 410 who had not been treated. Results indicated that the maltreatment did in fact have a significant negative influence on the children's performance in school. The maltreated children scored lower in test scores, especially in reading, and earned fewer A's and B's and more F's than children who had not been mistreated. In addition, children who have been maltreated are more likely to fail and repeat a grade. In fact, one out of every three abused and neglected children repeat at least one grade in elementary school.

A similar study in Georgia using a smaller population (21 physically abused, 47 neglected) and a non-matched control group compared test scores, grades, and teacher and parent interviews between the adjustment of maltreated children and those in the control groups. Abused and neglected children were more likely to demonstrate disturbed behaviors such as aggression,

---

* Adapted from *The Role of Educators in the Prevention and Treatment of Child Abuse and Neglect: The User Manual Series* (U.S. Department of Health and Human Services, 1992).

hyperactivity, anxiety, and depression. Maltreated children had lower self-concepts and felt unpopular in school. In addition, maltreated children scored significantly lower in language, math, and reading scores in the Iowa and Georgia Criterion Reference Test. Teachers felt these children were learning at below average levels and were more likely to repeat a grade.

Research also indicates that the child who is physically handicapped or mentally impaired is at a statistically greater risk of child abuse and neglect than the normal child. In some instances, the handicapped child may be viewed as a disappointment, a burden, or proof of parent "failure." Special educators should be sensitive to the particular stress that having a handicapped child can produce in some families. It is well known that children whose physical needs and problems are ignored may experience learning difficulties. Children who are always hungry or who cannot see the blackboard nor hear the teacher because they need glasses or hearing aids cannot learn well, and this inability to learn will be reflected in academic achievement.

Of course, academic difficulties may have a variety of causes and the presence of an academic problem does not prove that child abuse or neglect exists. But, the *possibility* of child abuse or neglect must be considered, along with other possible causes, when the problem is assessed.

Emotional/Psychological Clues

Educators are sensitive to children who are "different," e.g., physically or mentally disabled. That sensitivity can be extended to abused and neglected children, who may also appear to be different.

Educators must be alert to hostile and angry children who effectively alienate all who come in contact with them, or those who may be completely passive, withdrawn, and uncommunicative. These represent extremes in the expected range of behavior, attitude, and affect of abused and neglected children.

Sudden changes in children's emotional or psychological well-being may also serve as clues to child abuse and neglect. The previously gregarious children who are now uncommunicative might be concealing something upsetting.

Children are often barometers of family life: sunny when things are fine, stormy when they are not. A sudden change in the attitude or affect does not prove that child abuse and neglect exists. But maltreatment should be one of the possibilities considered when a problem situation is assessed.

Recognizing Child Abuse and Neglect through Interviews

Important information about a family can be gathered from routine conversations with parents and children. Parents and children often reveal details of family life, discuss methods of discipline, or directly ask for help with a problem when talking with a classroom teacher, school administrator, nurse, or counselor.

Conversations with the parent provide clues as to how the parent feels about the child. The presence of child abuse and neglect may be indicated if the parent constantly:

- blames or belittles the child
- sees the child as very different from his or her siblings in a negative way
- sees the child as "bad," "evil," or a "monster"
- finds nothing good or attractive in the child
- seems unconcerned about the child
- fails to keep appointments or refuses to discuss problems the child may be having in school
- misuses alcohol or other drugs and/or
- behaves in a bizarre and irrational way.

The educator who knows a child's family is in a better position to gauge whether a problem may be child abuse or neglect or something else, a chronic condition or temporary situation, something the school can readily handle or a problem that demands outside intervention.

Family circumstances may also provide clues regarding the possible presence of abuse or neglect. When a family is isolated from friends and neighbors or there is no apparent "life-line" to which a family can turn in times of crisis, the risk of abuse or neglect increases. Crisis in marital, economic, emotional, or social factors in a family should be assessed carefully as possible causes of family stress.

Sometimes when considering the possibility of child abuse and neglect, the educator may want to talk with the parent or child about a particular incident. Before having this talk, the educator must be convinced that such a conversation will not put the child in further danger. Such conversation is appropriate provided it is handled nonjudgmentally, carefully, and professionally.

Talking with the Child

While there are times when more information is needed to make a report to child protection services, it is the educator's role to report any suspicions of child abuse and neglect. However, it is the role of child protection services to conduct the investigation and talk to all parties to determine whether child abuse or neglect has occurred.

When determined necessary to talk with a child concerning a possible inflicted injury or neglectful condition, the educator must keep in mind the child may be hurt, in pain, fearful, or apprehensive. The child must be made as comfortable as possible in the circumstances.

The educator who talks with the child should be a person the child trusts and respects as well as the person most competent for interviewing children in the school. The educator interviewing the child may be joined by a colleague — groups of people should be avoided. When the principal insists on participating in the discussion, the effects on the child should be discussed with the principal first. The conversation should be conducted in a quiet, private, nonthreatening place, free of interruptions. The school library, a conference room, or an office are possible choices. The child would be put at ease, and that educator should sit near the child, not behind a desk or table.

Children should be assured they are not in trouble and they have done nothing wrong. Victimized children often feel or were told they are to blame for their own maltreatment and for bringing "trouble" to the family; therefore, it is important to reassure children they are not at fault.

The child should be assured the conversation will not be shared freely with other classmates and teachers. (If the educator feels the need to talk to a fellow teacher, this might not be mentioned to the child.) If maltreatment is suspected, the educator must remember that he or she *is* a mandated reporter and this must be explained to the child. It is easy to fall into the role of confidante to an abused child who has begged that no one be told. If educators tell children initially they must report to get help but will remain their supporter throughout the process, the abused child will feel more comfortable.

Use language a child can understand. When describing an abuse incident, if the educator is not familiar with a term the child uses, the educator should ask for an explanation or have the child point to the specific body part for clarification. The teacher should not disparage the child's choice of language; rather the interviewer should use the child's terms to put the child at ease and avoid confusion.

Educators are not inquisitors nor are they responsible for validating the abuse. Children should not be pressed for answers or details they are unwilling or unable to give. Answers should *not* be suggested to children and when enough information to make a report to child protection services has been gathered, the conversation should be concluded. The discussion need only gather. Educators can actually do more harm by probing for answers or supplying children with terms or information. Several major child sexual abuse cases have been dismissed in court because it was felt that the interviewers had biased the children.

If children wish to show their injuries to the educator, they should be allowed to do so. However, the educator should never insist on seeing the children's injuries. At no time should children be forced to remove clothing. It may be important to have the school nurse present should children decide to remove their clothes.

If further action is to be taken, the child should be told what will happen and when. The educator should assure the child of his or her support and assistance throughout the process and should follow through with assurances. Under no circumstances should the child be asked to conceal from the parents that the conversation has taken place or that further action is contemplated. Nor should the teacher display horror, anger, disgust, or disapproval of parents or the child.

It is important for the educator to be sensitive concerning the child's safety following the disclosure. If it is likely that the child will be vulnerable to parental abuse when he or she goes home and mentions telling someone at school, then child protection services should be called immediately. If the teacher feels the child may be in danger, he or she should mention this fact in the report. Support from child protection services may provide protection for the child.

If a child protection services caseworker needs to interview the child at school, the school should provide a private place for the interview and, if requested by the child, someone from the school whom the child trusts may be present throughout the interview. If it is necessary for the child protection services caseworker to remove the child from school for a medical examination, the school may request a written release from the caseworker. Many state and local child protection service agencies have established protocols with their respective school districts that outline procedures for interviewing children in schools.

Talking with the Parents

Many educators feel that it is important to contact parents to inform them that the school has made a report of suspected child abuse and neglect because they feel that contact will help maintain the parents' relationship with the school and keep the door open for further communication. It is never appropriate for educators to contact parents in an effort to "prove" a case of maltreatment by accusations or demands for explanation. If there are any repercussion concerns for the child's safety, it would be wise to discuss these with child protection services before scheduling a meeting with the parents.

Thought should be given to the most appropriate person to meet with the parents. In some cases, this may well be the classroom teacher. In others, the principal or a pupil-services staff member will be preferred. In still others, a combination of teachers and administrator or teacher and counselor is best. The principal must be included in any preparatory session before meeting with the parents.

Parents may be apprehensive or angry at the prospect of talking with the school about an injured or neglected child. It is important to make the parents feel as comfortable as possible. The conversation should be conducted in private and the parent should be told at the beginning that a report has been filed and there is legal authority for action.

In talking with the parents, the educator should respond in a professional, direct, and honest manner. If parents offer an explanation, the educator should be sympathetic. The teacher should never display anger, repugnance, or shock.

Parents should be assured of the confidentiality of the discussion but if some of what is discussed must be revealed to a third party such as child protection services, then this should be made clear. The educator should avoid prying into matters extraneous to the subject of the interview and should never betray the child's confidence to the parents.

The purpose of such a discussion is not only to notify parents that a report has been made but to assure them of the school's support for them and its continuing interest in the child. It is important not to alienate the family. Regardless of the outcome of the current situation, the school is likely to continue serving the family, perhaps for many years to come.

Occasionally, an angry parent will come to the school demanding to know why someone is "telling me how to raise my children." This is likely to happen particularly when the school has not informed the parent that it has filed a report of suspected child abuse or neglect. Parents have the right to know a report has been made. They often feel betrayed or that someone has "gone behind their back" when they are not told. Even though child protection services staff are mandated *not* to reveal the name of the referral source, the parents nearly always know where the report has come from and attempts at concealment only further anger them.

If angry parents appear at the school, they should be handled exactly as any other parent angry over any matter (for example a failing grade) is handled. In addition, the legal obligation to report should be stressed and the school's concern for the child reaffirmed.

Increasingly, schools are making it routine practice to notify parents when a report of suspected child abuse and neglect has been made by a staff member. The notification is firm but kind. It states the legal authority for the report and casts no blame. Parents are told to expect a visit from child protection services or other investigating agency and are offered support and concern.

Schools that have instituted this procedure report good results. Parents are less hostile and resentful when they understand that the school has a legal obligation it must fulfill. In addition, they often appreciate an expression, concern, or an offer of support at a time that, after all, is a difficult one.

Do's and Don'ts of Interviewing

The following summarizes the do's and don'ts of interviewing. Local schools may wish to add other items to these lists based on local policy and procedures.

When Talking with the Child DO . . .
- Make sure the educator is someone the child trusts.
- Make sure the educator is the person in the school most competent to talk with children.
- Conduct the discussion in private.
- Sit next to the child, not across the table.

- Tell the child the discussion is confidential but child abuse and neglect must be reported.
- Conduct the talk in language the child understands.
- Inform the child if future action will be required.

When Talking with the Child DON'T . . .
- Allow the child to feel "in trouble" or at "fault."
- Disparage or criticize the child's choice of words or language.
- Suggest answers to the child.
- Probe or press for answers the child is unwilling to give.
- Pressure or force the child to remove clothing.
- Conduct the discussion with a group of people.
- Leave the child alone with a stranger, such as a child protection services caseworker.

When Talking with the Parents DO . . .
- Select the person most appropriate to the situation.
- Conduct the discussion in private.
- Tell the parent(s) why the discussion is taking place.
- Be direct, honest, and professional.
- Confirm to the parent(s) if a report was made or will be made.
- Advise the parent(s) of the school's legal responsibilities to report.

When Talking with the Child DON'T . . .
- Try to prove abuse or neglect; that is not an educator's role.
- Display horror, shock, anger, or disapproval of the parent(s), child, or situation.
- Pry into family matters unrelated to the specific situation.
- Place blame or make judgments about the parent(s) or child.

Child Abuse Within the School

It is extremely disturbing for educators to consider that fellow colleagues could be abusing children. However, in the event this does occur, children need special protection. The usual response when educators suspect that one of their own is an abuser, especially if that person is a long-time employee, is to deny or even ignore the abuse. Sometimes the abuser is merely transferred to another school. Even with suspension or reprimand, violations are likely to re-cur in the absence of supervision and monitoring. In some instances the abuse continues under the enabling cover of the school for years. Educators owe children more protection than this.

If a child reports that he or she is being sexually, physically, or even emotionally abused by school personnel, the educator should remember that it takes courage for an abused child to talk to someone. The educator must consider facts and consistencies. Older children may invent stories but these usually contain obvious inconsistencies. First, the educator should determine if the child knows any other victims and, if so, should then talk with them. Alleged victims should be interviewed separately.

When a disclosure involves possible employee abuse, it is in the best interest of school districts to have policies and procedures already in place to be better able to protect both their students and employees by acting promptly in response to reported incidents. Such procedures should include disciplinary action when a district employee fails to report information about child abuse or maltreatment.

The school administrator (superintendent) must be notified and the situation should not be discussed among the other staff. The accused has a reputation and the right to know of the accusation. The investigator or principal should talk with the accused colleague early in the process. Not doing so often leads to a witch-hunt atmosphere and is not beneficial to students or faculty. Furthermore, it is unwise to ask children to tell their stories in front of the accused. There is a significant difference in power and resources between teachers and students.

In all cases it is crucial that allegations of abuse or neglect by an employee not lead to a resignation prior to a determination of a charge. In cases when resignations were permitted the employee has been known to move to another district without a record and thereby places other children at risk.

It is important to remember that schools are mandated reporters whether the abuser is an outsider or a school employee. Under state child abuse and neglect reporting statutes, educators have the same liabilities for failure to report suspected incidents perpetrated by colleagues as they would in incidents resulting from inter-familial abuse or neglect. If the abuse seems to have foundation, the police and/or child protection services must become involved. (In most states nonfamilial abuse is handled by the criminal justice system rather than child protection services.)

About Child Sexual Abuse*

Child sexual abuse is a problem that often can be stopped or avoided through education programs. Students can be empowered with knowledge and skills to help protect themselves from abuse. They can be taught how to recognize when someone is behaving in a way that suggests possible sexual abuse; to say no to secret, tricked, and unwanted touching; and get help from an adult to defend against future abuse.

---

*From Marjorie Fink, *Adolescent Sexual Assault and Harassment Prevention Curriculum* (Holmes Beach, Fla.: Learning Publications, 1995), 57-59.

The first step in any prevention program is empowering students with knowledge. Providing students with the following information will enable them to begin this process by helping them develop an understanding about child sexual abuse.

- Child sexual abuse is defined as the tricked, forced, and secret touching of a child's private parts under or through clothing. It may also be defined as any sexual contact with a child under a specific age (determined by state statutes) because a person under age is legally considered incapable of consent.

- Child sexual abuse includes any contacts or interactions between a child and an adult caretaker in which the child is being used for the sexual stimulation of the perpetrator or another person. Sexual abuse may also be committed by a person under the age of 18 when that person is either significantly older than the victim or when the perpetrator is in a position of power or control over the child.

- Child sexual abuse occurs in all social, economic, ethnic, and racial groups. Boys as well as girls are victims of sexual abuse. One out of every four females and one out of every seven males are sexually abused before 18 years of age. One-half of the victims are 12 and younger.

- Researchers believe that sexual abuse cases are under-reported. Boys in particular may under-report. Boys tend to be ashamed to admit that they did not protect themselves. Since boys usually are sexually abused by a male offender, they may perceive this act as a homosexual act and feel stigmatized.

- Children are sexually abused most often by a person whom they know and trust — usually someone in the family. In 90 percent of the cases, the abuser is someone whom the child knows. In over 60 percent of the cases, the abuser is the child's father or stepfather.

- Child sexual abuse usually occurs without force. The offender is often a person whom the child knows. Because there is an established relationship, the offender is able to take advantage of the child's trust and affection. Once the sexual activity occurs, the offender entraps the child by threatening him or her into keeping it a secret.

- Sexual abuse of children often continues for a number of years before detection. This occurs when the offender has continued access to the child who has been threatened into keeping it a secret. During this time, the sexual acts may progress from fondling to other acts including penetration.

- More than one child in a family may be the victim of sexual abuse. This may happen either concurrently or at different times, as one sibling grows up or leaves the home. Usually the children do not know about each other's victimization because the offender threatens each child to secrecy.

- It is a myth that children are seductive and willingly participate in or invite sexual behavior with adults. Seductive behavior is learned behavior that the child may use to gain attention and affection. When children exhibit seductive behavior it is because they are imitating adults and/or because the behavior is encouraged by the abuser. Regardless of whether or not the child acts seductively, it is the adult's responsibility not to engage in sexual activity of any kind with a child. Children are not mature enough to consent to sex. Therefore, the abused child is never at fault.

- Both male and female victims suffer trauma from sexual abuse. The trauma is caused by being betrayed, exploited, and misused. When a child is sexually abused, the level of psychological trauma is increased if (1) the child had an emotional or familial attachment to the abuser, (2) the abuse occurred over a long period of time, and (3) the child did not receive emotional support from a non-abusing parent or caretaker.

- Eighty percent of convicted child molesters were themselves molested when they were children. Underlying feelings of inadequacy and of "powerlessness" among their peers often cause molesters to turn to children to fill their emotional and psychological needs. Sexual abuse is the abuse of power by an older, bigger person who takes advantage of this relationship.

- Family factors can play a part in the beginning and continuation of child sexual abuse. Some factors that often exist in the home to create an environment allowing offenders to carry out the abuse are (1) poor patterns of communication, (2) a poor marital relationship, (3) role reversal between mother and daughter, and (4) family isolation and substance abuse.

- Child molesters almost never self-correct. Research suggests that most child molesters do not recognize their problem and will not seek help on their own. Without restraint or treatment, the rate of repeat offenses for offenders is extremely high. Reporting will help get abusers and victims into treatment. When the offender is in treatment, the family members must receive help in order to encourage the development of healthy patterns of interaction.

Child Sexual Abuse Prevention Concepts*

Review the following concepts with students emphasizing they are used in developing programs for young children. You also should discuss how these concepts apply to any age, including high school students.

- Children need self-esteem reinforcement in order to have the desire and confidence to take care of themselves.

---

*From Marjorie Fink, *Adolescent Sexual Assault and Harassment Prevention Curriculum* (Holmes Beach, Fla.: Learning Publications, 1995), 59-60.

- Children need to learn the importance of trusting and paying attention to their feelings.

- There are different kinds of touches: good, bad, and confusing. Different touches result in different feelings.

- Children need to know their bodies belong to them. No one has the right to touch them in ways that make them feel uncomfortable. It's okay to say no to adults or to anyone who makes them feel uncomfortable in any way.

- The way children say no is important. They need to practice saying no in different ways and in a loud, assertive voice. This may stop a sexually abusive situation and keep it from recurring.

- No one has the right to ask or tell a child to keep an unpleasant secret or a secret that makes the child feel bad. Children need to understand the difference between good secrets and secrets that should be told.

- Frequently, children feel guilty after a disclosure, especially when they did not resist or were ineffective in resisting sexual abuse. They need to hear from adults that they did the right thing by telling and that it's not their fault.

- Children need to think about, identify, and practice verbalizing the names of the people they could trust and tell if they have a problem.

- Children need to practice telling a trusted adult and keep telling until someone believes and helps them. This may keep a sexually abusive situation from recurring.

Resources

Child Abuse Recommended Resources

Besharov, Douglas J. *Recognizing Child Abuse: A Guide for the Concerned.* New York: Free Press, 1990. A good professional overview of child sexual abuse including the legal framework and the reporting process.

Camille, Pamela. *Step on a Crack (You Break Your Father's Back).* Colorado: Freedom Lights Press, 1988. The courageous story of a molested child and her recovery with emphasis on the importance of telling and getting help. It is written in the first person in a narrative form.

Daugherty, Lynn B. *Why Me? Help for Victims of Child Sexual Abuse (Even if They Are Adults Now).* Wisconsin: Mother Courage Press, 1984. Includes questions and answers about child sexual abuse, understanding people who sexually abuse children, stories of victims, effects on victims and their families, and a guide to recovery.

Faller, Kathleen Coulborn. *Child Sexual Abuse: Intervention and Treatment Issues.* Washington, D.C.: U.S. Department of Health and Human Services, 1993. Includes techniques for the child interview, substantiating sexual abuse, treatment modalities, and issues of child sexual abuse.

Finkelhor, David, and Associates. *A Sourcebook on Child Sexual Abuse.* Thousand Oaks, Calif.: Sage Publications, 1986. Provides theoretical and research material on the nature of child sexual abuse, its dynamics, and the larger forces shaping public and professional attitudes.

Howard, Judy. "Incest," *Teen Magazine* (July 1985). Excellent article for students includes stories of victims and stresses the importance of breaking the conspiracy of silence for the victim, the family, and in society.

Nelson, Mary, and Kay Clark, eds. *The Educator's Guide to Preventing Child Sexual Abuse.* Santa Cruz: Network Publications, 1986. Topics include issues on child sexual abuse prevention, guidelines for prevention education, and an overview of prevention programs at work.

Sgroi, Suzanne M. *Handbook of Clinical Intervention in Child Sexual Abuse.* Lexington, Mass.: Lexington Books, D.C. Heath and Company, 1982. A collection of articles written by experts in the field of child sexual abuse covering the topics of validation and treatment.

Tower, C.C. *The Role of Educators in the Prevention of Child Abuse and Neglect.* Washington, D.C.: U.S. Department of Health and Human Services for Children and Families, 1992. Includes local policy procedures regarding reporting and information on state laws.

Vanderbilt, Heide. "Incest: A Chilling Report," *Lear's* (February 1992): 49-77. An extremely powerful and informative article about incest. One of the most comprehensive of its kind. Strongly recommended for educators.

Child Sexual Abuse Prevention Videos

Child Sexual Abuse: A Solution. James Stansfield Pub. Co., P.O. Box 41058, Santa Barbara, CA 93140. VHS 1/2" cassette, 15 minutes each part. This six-part filmstrip series on video for children and teachers is designed to separately address different age groups. Part 1 features a cartoon about Chester the Cat that effectively reinforces prevention concepts for young children. Suggested for grades K-6.

Don't Touch. Select Media, 60 Warren St., Suite 5A, New York, NY 10007. VHS 1/2" cassette, 31 minutes, (800) 707-6334. This sensitively presented program is a moving, dramatic portrayal that clearly shows the seductive process present in the sexual abuse of young children. It also stresses the importance of telling and getting help even if the abuse has long stopped. Suggested for grades 5-12.

Listen to Me: Physical Child Abuse. Coronet/MTI Film and Video, 4350 Equity Dr., Columbus, OH 43228. VHS 1/2" cassette, 22 minutes, (800) 621-2131. This sensitive dramatization explores the problem of physical child abuse from the child's perspective, teaching viewers how to distinguish between discipline and abuse. It emphasizes the importance of getting help for family members when child abuse is a problem in the family.

No More Secrets. Select Media, 60 Warren St., Suite 5A, New York, NY 10007. VHS 1/2" cassette, 13 minutes, (800) 707-6334. Four friends talk over sexually abusive experiences they've had with family members. Problem solving and skills for prevention and protection are highlighted in the children's conversations. Suggested for grades 4-6.

A Touchy Subject. Select Media, 60 Warren St., Suite 5A, New York, NY 10007. VHS 1/2" cassette, 26 minutes, (800) 707-6334. An excellent video for schools to use with parents. Four short dramatic scenes depict parents talking to children of various ages about the prevention of child sexual abuse.

Who Should You Tell? Dealing with Abuse. Sunburst Communications, Pleasantville, NY 10570. VHS 1/2" cassette, 14 minutes, (800) 431-1934. Karen, a fifth-grade victim of child sexual abuse, is the film's narrator. Through her voice she is able to identify common feelings, fears, and perceptions of young people dealing with this situation. It also effectively reinforces the concepts that no one should keep scary secrets, the importance of telling an adult, and getting help. Suggested for grades 4-6.

Yes, You Can Say No. Committee for Children, 172 20th Ave., Seattle, WA 98122. VHS 1/2" cassette, 19 minutes, (206) 322-5050. David is being sexually exploited by a once-trusted adult. Drawing on his own resources and those of his friends, David learns the assertiveness skills necessary to resist and report abuse. Suggested for grades 4-6.

Child Sexual Abuse Prevention Children's Books and Educator's Resources

About Telling. The Rhode Island Chapter of the National Committee for the Prevention of Child Abuse, (401) 728-7920. An excellent coloring activity book that reinforces the importance of telling a trusted adult when you have a problem. It also reinforces the concepts that your body is your own, you can say no, and you should not keep secrets about touching. Suggested for grades 3-4.

The Amazing Spider-Man: Spider-Man and Power Pack Child Sexual Abuse Prevention Comic Books. Chicago: NCPCA Publishing. Comic book format. Stresses belief that children are not powerless against sexual abuse. Deals with how children protect themselves by saying no and telling someone, and that it's never a child's fault. Suggested for grades 4-6.

Fink, Marjorie. *Protecting Children from Sexual Abuse.* Huntington, N.Y.: The Bureau for At-Risk Youth, 1992. This is a resource for parents in pamphlet form. It can be handed out at parent education programs or made available during the implementation of a school's child sexual abuse prevention program. It covers preventing sexual abuse: what to teach your child, what parents can do, and how to help a child who has been abused.

Freeman, Lory. *It's My Body: A Book to Teach Young Children How to Resist an Uncomfortable Touch.* Seattle: Parenting Press, 1980. Available through KidsRights catalogue, (800) 892-KIDS. Picture book with simple language that teaches children the difference between good and bad touches, and their right to say no to uncomfortable touches. Suggested for Preschool – grade 1.

Girard, Linda. *My Body is Private.* Niles, Ill.: Alberty Whitman & Co. Available through KidsRights catalogue, 1-800-892-KIDS. Picture and story book clarifying the meaning of private, privacy, private parts, and different kinds of touches. Also emphasizes saying no and telling someone. Can be read to children in grades 1-2 and read by children in grades 3-4.

Good Touch, Bad Touch: An Educational Coloring and Activities Book. Flushing, N.Y.: Promotional Slideguide, 1996. 718-886-8408. A coloring book that teaches the difference between good and bad touches and a child's right to say no to bad touches. Suggested for grades K-2.

He Told Me Not To Tell. Renton, Wash.: King County Rape Relief, 1979. Suggestions for parents or teachers on how to discuss sexual assault with children and how to help them learn to protect themselves. Includes activities that teach prevention skills.

Plummer, Carol. *Preventing Sexual Abuse: Activities and Strategies for Those Working with Children and Adolescents.* Second ed. Holmes Beach, Fla.: Learning Publications, 1997, (800) 222-1525. This step-by-step multi-level curriculum guide is organized in five-day and three-day presentations for K-grade 6 or the developmentally disabled, and five-day or three-day presentations, or a one-day sessions for grades 7–12.

Proud to Be Me: A Self-Esteem Coloring and Activities Book. Flushing, N.Y.: Promotional Slideguide, 1996. (718) 886-8408. This is a self-esteem coloring book appropriate for younger children. It reinforces the concept that it is our differences that makes us all special.

Wachter, Oralee. *No More Secrets.* New York: Little Brown and Co., 1984. Available through KidsRights catalogue, 1-800-892-KIDS. Episodic format in four stories about children involving privacy and touching private parts, saying no, and telling someone. Stories can be adapted for role playing and skits with other children. Suggested for ages 8 and up.

You're in Charge. South Deerfield, Mass.: Channing L. Bete Co., 1990. (800) 628-7733. A coloring book that teaches the difference between good and bad touches and a child's right to say no to bad touches. Suggested for grades 3-4.

Unit 1: Child Sexual Abuse Prevention

Part B: Classroom Materials

Child Sexual Abuse Prevention
Curriculum for Grades K-3

Goals

■ Students will learn that there are different kinds of touches: good, bad, confusing; and that different touches result in different feelings.

■ Students will learn the importance of paying attention to their feelings and trust them.

■ Students will learn that their bodies belong to them. No one has a right to touch them in ways that make them feel uncomfortable.

■ Students will learn that it's OK to say no to adults, their peers, or anyone who makes them feel uncomfortable in any way. They will learn the importance of saying no in different ways and in a loud, assertive voice.

■ Students will learn the importance of telling a trusted adult to get help when they have been improperly touched, or hurt, or made to feel uncomfortable. They will learn that it's never their fault if they get a bad touch. They will also learn to keep telling a trusted adult until someone believes and helps them.

Introduce Topic

Before covering the topic of sexual abuse prevention, involve the students in a self-esteem activity. Children need self-esteem reinforcement to encourage them to want to take care of themselves and give them the confidence to do it. This is important not only to strengthen self-boundaries and help children develop a sense of self-identity but to see that "self" as special, unique, worthy, and of value.

Discussing feelings are also an important part of sexual abuse prevention because children need to learn to trust their feelings in situations that involve tricked, secret, or forced touching. Through activities that discuss feelings children can be encouraged to listen to their feelings, trust how they feel, and be helped to make the connection between touches and feelings.

Explain that one important way to take care of yourself involves deciding how you are touched and treated. Although most kids do not experience bad touches, those who were touched in ways that made them feel bad and uncomfortable said that when they knew what to do about a bad touch it really helped them feel safe.

Classroom Activities

1. **Everyone Is Special.** This provides a self-esteem activity that encourages children to see themselves as special because they are unique and different. It encourages children to think about the ways they take care of their

special selves, that their bodies are special, and that their feelings are a special part of them too.

2. **Different Touches/Different Feelings.** This activity helps children understand the difference between good, bad, and confusing touches; that different touches result in different feelings; and the importance of listening to your feelings about touching. It also provides an activity using a video to teach and reinforce the concepts that your body belongs to you, you can decide who touches you, and it's OK to say no to anyone about touches you don't like.

3. **You Can Say No.** This activity reinforces the assertive skill of saying no. It provides specific "what-if" situations related to touching, tricks, bribes, privacy, and secrets. Students practice saying no in different ways and in loud, assertive voices.

4. **You Can Tell.** This activity develops the assertive skill of asking for help. It provides an opportunity for the students to practice identifying a trusted adult and "telling."

Activity 1 – Everyone is Special

Empowering children through enhancing their self-esteem can help reduce their vulnerability to sexual assault. Using one activity alone cannot accomplish this but it can provide a positive way to introduce the topic and it does set the tone to encourage children to see themselves as special, unique, and deserving of good treatment. Providing self-esteem reinforcement on a daily basis can help give children the confidence they need to protect themselves.

The following are some ways educators can accomplish this:

- Emphasize the value of being different and, therefore, special by helping children appreciate and understand the differences in people.
- Stress the ways we take care of our special selves in terms of health, nutrition, and safety.
- Provide children with acceptable choices about touching and privacy, the opportunity to make their own decisions, learning to assert themselves.
- Reinforce the meaning of privacy, private possessions, and caring for one's own possessions. Encourage pride in ownership, respect for property, and the right to privacy. Children can then apply this concept to their own bodies.

The Magic Box

Begin the activity by telling the children that you have a magic box. "Each of you will have a chance to look inside the box and see the most important person in the world. In fact, there is no one else like this person in the whole world." When each child looks inside the box ask, "Who do you see?" When they respond "me" then say, "That's right you are really special." Tell each child to keep secret what they've seen so every child gets a chance to be surprised.

After everyone has a turn to peek into the Magic Box reinforce the following:

■ We are all special because we are all different from each other. Elicit responses from students about the ways they are different from each other.

■ Explain that it is important to take care of yourselves and your bodies because they belong to you and are special too.

■ Our feelings, like our bodies, are an important part of us and are special too.

Feelings Are Important

While doing a feeling activity reinforce the following reasons why our feelings are an important part of all of us:

■ Our feelings help us by letting us know if what is happening feels good or bad.

■ By paying attention to our feelings we can then decide if anything needs to be done to help us feel better.

■ Only you know how you feel. If something feels funny, does not feel OK or feels bad, then you are right.

Involve the children in an activity that encourages them to name the different ways people feel and identify different situations that make them feel that way such as:

Have children act out their feelings after throwing feeling dice, picking a feeling card, playing feeling bingo, or using a sock puppet.

Feeling Dice: Make large dice out of heavy construction paper. Attach to each surface of the dice the simple picture faces below depicting different facial expressions. Have children act out their feelings after throwing feeling dice.

Feelings Cards: Make cards with the simple picture faces below depicting different facial expressions. A variation of this is to cut out pictures from the newspapers or magazines showing the facial expressions of different people. Have children act out their feelings after picking a card.

Feeling Bingo: Make a bingo card using the simple faces depicted below. Make a circle spinner with these faces. When it lands on a face have the children place a marshmallow on the square and give students turns saying what makes them feel angry, sad, etc. After all the squares are covered the children get to eat the marshmallows off the card.

Sock Puppet: Give the students turns using a sock puppet to act out feelings. Have a student in the class guess the feeling being acted out and then ask him or her to give an example of what makes them feel that way.

Some examples of easy faces that can be drawn to be used with these activities are:

Happy   **Sad**   **Scared**   **Surprised**   **Angry**

Proud to Be Me

This self-esteem coloring book, annotated in the Unit 1A references, is appropriate for younger children and reinforces the concept that it is our differences that make us all special. An activity that can follow the coloring book or stand on it's own would be to make classroom posters reflecting the children's differences in the class. For example one page in the coloring book says, "kids come in all colors." This could be the heading of the poster that contains pictures of the children in the class. The bottom of the poster can say, "We are all different and special." Other examples of poster ideas from the coloring book:

- Kids live in different kinds of houses
- Kids like all kinds of different foods
- Kids have different kinds of families
- Kids enjoy different kinds of activities

Activity 2 – Different Touches/Different Feelings

Good, Bad, and Confusing Touches

Ask the students for examples of good, bad, and confusing touches. Then define and emphasize that each person knows whether a touch is good, bad, or confusing by how it makes you feel. It is very important to listen to your feelings about touching and trust your feelings:

Good Touch: This is a touch that feels good like a handshake or a hug that you want. You know it's a good touch because it feels good.

Bad Touch: This is a touch that feels bad such as a hit, a punch, or a kick. It is also when someone tricks you into touching the private parts of your body (the parts covered by a bathing suit). Anytime someone touches you and tells you to keep it a secret that is always a bad touch. You know it's a bad touch because it hurts or feels bad.

Confusing Touch: This is when you are not sure whether the touch was good or bad. It is confusing because the person who is touching you is someone you know and trust. You know it's a confusing touch because you feel "Uh-oh. Something is not right."

Emphasize:

■ No one has a right to touch you in ways that make you feel uncomfortable.

■ Different touches result in different feelings. You know what kind of touch it is by how you feel about it. You know its a good touch because it feels good. You know it's a bad touch because it hurts or feels bad. You know it's a confusing touch because you feel "Uh-oh. Something is not right."

■ Listen to your feelings about touching. If you feel funny or bad about someone touching you or seeing your body without clothes, your feelings are telling you no I don't like this. Whenever you feel this way — say no, get away, and tell an adult about it.

■ It is never a child's fault. It is always wrong for a bigger or older person to trick or force a child into getting a bad touch.

Video: *Child Sexual Abuse: A Solution**

Grades K-1: This part of the video shows a cartoon about Chester the Cat. Chester gets lots of touches he doesn't like from his friends because he has a most extraordinary tail that everyone likes to touch.

Review the following concepts emphasized in the video:

• Your body belongs to you

• You can decide who touches you.

• You can say no even to someone bigger than you about touches you don't like.

• The way you say no is important. Use your important voice to say no so they will know you really mean it.

Give each child a picture of an animal to color in and tell them to make one part of the animal very special, such as special ears for a rabbit. The children can then take turns acting out their animals and role play using their important voice to say no to touches they don't like. Then create a book of all the animals for each child to take home. Keep a copy for the classroom library for reinforcement.

Grades 2-3: Show the cartoon about Chester the Cat and present the "what-if" situations in part 2 of the video.

Review the concepts listed above and the following additional concepts:

• It's not your fault if someone gives you a bad touch even if you didn't say no or promised not to tell.

• Keep telling adults you trust until you get help.

Have each child draw his or her own animal with a special part. Children can write a story about protecting the part of the body that their animal

---

**Child Sexual Abuse: A Solution.* Available from James Stansfield Pub. Co., P.O. Box 41058, Santa Barbara, CA 93140. VHS 1/2" cassette, 15 minutes each part.

friend's like to touch. They can also act out their animals and role play using their important voice to remind their friends their body belongs to them, they can decide who touches them, and they can say no to touches they don't like. Then create a book of all the animal stories for the class.

Activity 3 – You Can Say No

Adults have power over children because they are taught to obey adult authority. A child who is never allowed to say no to an authority figure is unlikely to be assertive in a threatening situation even if the child understands the importance of saying no. Because it is so difficult for children to stand up to adults and say no, especially in an assaultive situation, they need to practice saying no in a loud, assertive voice and in different ways. This may stop a sexually abusive situation and stop it from recurring.

When empowering children with their right to say no, emphasize the following:

- It is OK to say no to adults or anyone who makes you feel uncomfortable in any way even if it's someone in your family, a teacher, your coach — anyone!

- When someone makes you feel bad and you need to tell them no, say it in your loudest voice so they know you really mean it.

- Always say no in a very loud voice whenever someone tries to trick you into touching the private parts of your body and anytime someone says the touching is a secret.

- It is OK to say no when you want your body to be private and you don't want anyone to see your body while you are dressing, when you are bathing, or in the bathroom.

Saying No Role-Play Game

In this activity students will each have a chance while playing a game to practice using their important voice to say no to bad touches. All kinds of bad touches are included, not just examples involving sexual abuse, because children need to practice asserting themselves with adults and their peers in everyday life experiences so they can be prepared to use this skill to protect themselves.

Prepare two sets of index cards. One set has written examples of touches that kids may experience in their daily lives in their interaction with their peers. If the students are old enough, they may generate the examples from their own experiences. The other set of cards contains examples involving touching of private parts, secret touching, and tricked touching by someone older and bigger.

Review the following things each student in the group can do to assert themselves or "show they really mean it":

- Use your most important voice.
- Stand up straight and tall.
- Have a serious expression on your face.
- Look the person in the eyes.
- Say what you want over and over again until they believe you.

Then give each child two turns. Instruct the children to pick one card from each pile and encourage them to assert themselves and "show they really mean it" and tell the class "what would you say if someone tried to . . . " (use the example from the card picked by the child).

Examples for one card pile. Reinforce the message, "It's your body. No one has a right to hurt you!"

What would you do if someone tried to . . .

- pull your hair in class?
- push you while walking in the hall?
- hit you on the playground?
- trip you on purpose?
- pinch you?

Examples for the second card pile. Reinforce, "Your body belongs to you. You can decide who looks at your body. You can decide who touches you. It's always a bad touch and very important to say no when it's secret or tricked touching."

What would you do if someone tried to . . .

- peek at you while you are undressing and you want privacy?
- play a secret touching game with you?
- give you a present if you take off your clothes?
- touch a private part of your body and tell you to keep it a secret?
- offer to buy you a toy if you let them touch you?

Encourage the students to practice asserting themselves and to practice saying no whenever they need to with their classmates. Suggest that as the school year progresses, more cards can be added to the pile from things that happen in school and the class can play the game and practice again.

Explain to the students that although it feels good to learn how to take care of yourself and how to say no to protect your body, it is also very important to tell a trusted adult and get help if you get a bad touch or if you feel uncomfortable in any way.

Activity 4 – You Can Tell

It is important for children to learn how to protect themselves since it is likely they will be alone with the abuser. However, you can only really ensure a child's safety from further abuse if an adult assumes responsibility for the child's protection. Children need a great deal of encouragement to tell because they may have promised not to tell, they may have been told what happened was their fault, and they may not know how or who to tell.

While proceeding with the activities, emphasize the following to enable children to tell and get the help they need:

■ Sometimes it's hard to tell if you promised not to tell or if you think the touching was your fault.

■ It is never a child's fault even if they promised not to tell and even if they didn't say no. It is always wrong for a bigger and older person to trick or force a child into getting a bad touch.

■ Remember, it is always OK to tell a bad secret to get help (a bad secret is any secret about touching or any secret that makes you feel bad).

■ It's always OK to tell a trusted adult if you need help and its very important to keep telling until you get help.

■ If you come to me for help I will believe you, I will not blame you, and I will help you be safe.

■ Encourage the students to think about whom they would tell in their family and in the community if they needed help. It is also important to identify the people in school who could be trusted and helpful.

Who Would You Tell?

This activity provides the students with an opportunity to choose whom they would tell if they needed help with touching and to practice telling an adult.

Give each child the Grownups Who Can Help handout in this activity. Ask them to color in or circle one person in the family, the community, and in the school whom they could tell if they needed help. Then present the same situations used to practice saying no.

For Grades K-1: Explain to the children that they worked hard at saying no to bad touches. Now they each will have a turn practicing whom they would tell if they needed help.

Have the students look at their handouts and ask who would you tell if someone tried to . . .

• play a secret touching game with you?

• give you a present if you take off your clothes?

• touch a private part of your body and tell you to keep it a secret?

• buy you a toy if you let them touch you?

42

- made you promise not to tell and you promised?

After everyone has a turn saying who they would tell ask them to circle one more person in their family, community, and school. Just in case the first person they tell is not able to help, they need to think about who else to tell to get help.

For Grades 2-3: Proceed with the activity as outlined above. In addition, instruct the students to identify the pictures of the people in the handout by name that they could tell.

Ask the students to then role play telling a trusted adult using the situations suggested above. The teacher assumes the role of the person they chose to tell and responds by saying what the students need to hear to encourage telling: I believe you. It's not your fault. I'm glad you told me. It's OK to tell bad secrets and to tell even though you promised not to. I am glad you kept telling and I will help you.

As a class project, make a poster with the heading People You Can Tell If You Need Help. Have each child contribute several people they identified in their handout to display in the classroom on the communal poster.

Then Say No, Get Away, and Tell Someone Game

This is an effective final activity because it reinforces the concepts of prevention taught throughout the program.

Use the classroom corners as an interactive game board. Each child takes a turn and proceeds clockwise around the room. Hang up signs in each corner indicating the following:

Corner #1 - The Starting Line   Corner #3 - Get Away
Corner #2 - Say No   Corner #4 - Tell Someone

When a child takes a turn, present one of the following what-if situations and ask the child all the questions listed below to guide them along the game board (the corners of the room).

1. At the starting line ask, What if someone tried to . . .
   - peek at you while you are undressing and you want privacy?
   - play a secret touching game with you?
   - give you a present if you take off your clothes?
   - touch a private part of your body and tell you to keep it a secret?
   - offer to buy you a toy if you let them touch you?

2. What should you say? (Encourage the child to say no loudly and move to the Say No corner.)

3. What should you do then? (Encourage the child to run fast to the Get Away Corner.)

4. Who would you tell? (Encourage the child to name a trusted adult.)

5. What would you say? (The child should go to the Tell Someone corner and be encouraged to say, "I need help. Someone tried to give me a bad touch.")

When each child completes their turn they should be told "good job at saying no, getting away, and telling." If possible give some form of positive reinforcement such as a happy face sticker or pin, a "say no, get away, tell someone good job "award."

Resources

The following materials, annotated in the references, effectively reinforce the prevention concepts already covered and can provide an opportunity to involve parents. Choose one that is age appropriate and provide for the students to complete with an adult at home. Review the completed books in class.

- *Good Touch, Bad Touch: An Educational Coloring and Activities Book* (Grades K-2).
- *You're in Charge* (Grades 3-4)
- *About Telling* (Grades 3-4)

Grandmother or Grandfather

Doctor

Sister

Nurse

Police

Father

Teacher

Teacher

Social Worker

Mother

Brother

Child Sexual Abuse Prevention Curriculum for Grades 4-6

Goals

- Students will learn that there are different kinds of touches: good, bad, and confusing; and that different touches result in different feelings.

- Students will learn the importance of paying attention to their feelings and to trust them.

- Students will learn that their bodies belong to them. No one has a right to touch them in ways that make them feel uncomfortable.

- Students will learn that it's OK to say no to adults, their peers, or anyone who makes them feel uncomfortable in any way. They will learn the importance of saying no in different ways and in a loud, assertive voice.

- Students will learn the importance of telling a trusted adult to get help with touching, if someone hurts them or makes them feel uncomfortable. They will learn that it's never their fault if they get a bad touch. They will also learn to keep telling until a trusted adult believes and helps them.

Introduce Topic

If possible, before covering the topic of sexual abuse prevention involve the students in a self-esteem activity. This is important in order to encourage them to want to take care of themselves and give them the confidence to do it. A simple but effective activity is to ask the students to each look in a mirror. They will see someone that is unique and different from anyone else in the whole wide world. Then reinforce with the students: "You are all very special. There is no one else exactly like you. Our differences make us special." Encourage them to take care of their special selves: "It is important to take good care of yourself because you all deserve good treatment."

We are going to learn that one important way to take care of yourself involves deciding how you are touched and treated. Although most kids do not experience bad touches, those who were touched in ways that made them feel bad and uncomfortable said that when they knew what to do about a bad touch. It really helped them feel safe. We are going to learn about good touches and bad touches so that you can be safe too.

Touching children on the private parts of their body (the parts covered by a bathing suit) is against the law in this country. Laws protect our rights. Can you think of what other rights we have? Encourage the students to include the right to an education, freedom of speech, to own personal property, not to be hurt by others, and to think and feel anything they want. We are fortunate to live in this country and have our rights protected. This is not true everywhere in the world.

Before continuing with the classroom activities ask the students for examples of good, bad, and confusing touches. Then define and emphasize that each person knows whether a touch is good, bad, or confusing by how it makes you feel. It is important to listen to your feelings about touching and trust your feelings.

Good Touch: This is a touch that feels good like a handshake or a hug that you want. You know its a good touch because it feels good.

Bad Touch: This is a touch that feels bad such as a hit, a punch, or a kick. It is also when someone tricks you into touching the private parts of your body. Also anytime someone touches you and tells you to keep it a secret that is always a bad touch. You know it's a bad touch because it hurts or feels bad.

Confusing Touch: This is when you are not sure whether the touch was good or bad. It is confusing because the person who is touching you is someone you know and trust. You know it's a confusing touch because you feel "Uh-oh. Something is not right."

Classroom Activities

5. **Video: *No More Secrets*:** This is an excellent resource in which four friends tell their stories about touching and lack of privacy. It covers the concepts of good, bad, and confusing touches, saying no loudly, the importance of asserting oneself, it's never a child's fault, trusting your feelings, and of telling and getting help.

6. **Scenarios for Discussion and Role Play:** Scenarios are provided as examples of the most typical kinds of child sexual abuse or potentially abusive situations. They provide an opportunity for fuller discussion and reinforcement of learned skills.

7. **Student Response Form:** This activity develops the assertive skill of asking for help. It provides an opportunity for the students to identify grown-ups they could trust if they had a problem with touching or privacy. It also provides students with an opportunity to ask their teacher in private questions about the program and to ask for help if they need it.

Activity 5 – Video: *No More Secrets**

Before showing the video explain that it is about four friends who share concerns with each other about being touched or treated in ways that made them feel uncomfortable. Ask the students to think about how each person felt when describing what happened to them. Then ask the students to think about how their feelings changed once they learned how to protect themselves.

Discuss the first situation:
- How did the girl feel about her friend taking her diary?
- What right was taken away from her?
- How did she feel when her brother peeked at her taking a shower?
- What did her friends tell her to do? When she said no in a big voice why was this helpful?
- How did her feelings change when she decided to stand up to her brother?
- How did this help her get her diary back? Describe.

Discuss the second situation:
- What kind of touch is this an example of? (Confusing touch)
- How did it make him feel?
- Why did the boy think it was his fault? (He thought it was his fault because he didn't say no. This is a good time to emphasize that it is never a child's fault even if they didn't say no or promised not to tell.)
- What else should he do to be safe besides telling his uncle that he doesn't like the way his uncle touches him? (Always tell an adult. If he handles it himself he will worry about it happening again.)
- How did he feel when he learned what to do about his uncle's touching?

Discuss the third situation:
- Which one is the most difficult situation to talk about? (Being touched by a family member.)
- How did she feel about being touched by her father at night when he tucked her in?
- Why did she blame herself? (Because she promised not to tell. Again emphasize that it's never a child's fault.)
- Why did her friends tell her to keep telling an adult she trusts until

---

*No More Secrets as well as other videos are listed in the resources in Unit 1A.

someone believes her?

- How did she feel after her friends supported her and she decided to get help?

After discussing the video, inform the students that it is important to practice saying no and telling. Then proceed to the Scenarios for Discussion and Role Play Activity and the Student Survey.

Activity 6 – Scenarios for Discussion and Role Play

Most scenarios are appropriate for grades 4–6. The presenter should make choices based on the students' level of maturity and prior understanding of the concepts. The scenarios provided are examples of the most typical kinds of child sexual abuse or potentially abusive situations. They provide an opportunity for fuller discussions, new insights, and reinforcement of learned skills. Skill development should be stressed here. Most students have an understanding of concepts but need practice saying no assertively and getting help.

Present each scenario to the class for discussion purposes. During the discussion provide the students with information and reinforcement of prevention concepts.

When empowering children with their right to say no, emphasize the following:

- It is OK to say no to adults or anyone who makes you feel uncomfortable in any way even if it's someone in your family, a teacher, your coach — anyone!

- When someone makes you feel bad and you need to tell them no, say it in your loudest voice so they know you really mean it.

- Always say no in a loud voice whenever someone tries to trick you into touching the private parts of your body and anytime someone says the touching is a secret.

- It is OK to say no when you want your body to be private and you don't want anyone to see your body while you are dressing, when you are bathing, or in the bathroom.

Following the discussion for each scenario, role plays are provided that give the students an opportunity to role play saying no assertively. Because it is so difficult for children to stand up to adults and say no especially in an assaultive situation, they need to practice saying no in a loud, assertive voice and in different ways. This may stop a sexually abusive situation and keep it from recurring. Review the Assertiveness Techniques (Handout #2) and explain that these are things you can do to help assert yourself in order to be taken seriously when you say no. Refer to these techniques during the role play.

Following the discussion for each situation provide the students with an opportunity to role play getting help. It is important for children to learn how to protect themselves since it is likely they will be alone with the abuser. However, you can only really ensure a child's safety from further abuse if an adult assumes responsibility for the child's protection. Children need a great deal of encouragement to tell because they may have promised not to tell, they may have been told what happened was their fault, and they may not know how or who to tell.

While proceeding with the activities emphasize the following to enable children to tell and get the help they need:

- Sometimes it hard to tell if you promised not to tell or if you think the touching was your fault.

- It is never a child's fault even if you promised not to tell and even if you didn't say no. It is always wrong for a bigger and older person to trick or force a child into getting a bad touch.

- Remember, it is always OK to tell a bad secret to get help. (A bad secret is any secret about touching, any secret that makes you feel bad.)

- It's always OK to tell a trusted adult if you need help and its important to keep telling until you get help.

- If you come to me for help I will believe you, I will not blame you, and I will help you be safe.

- Encourage the students to think about whom they would tell in their family and in the community if they needed help. It is also important to identify the people in school who could be trusted and helpful.

Scenario # 1

When Donna is in her room alone her brother walks in without knocking. He even does it when she is dressing. She told him to stop but he says, "Oh, I forgot." She feels he does it on purpose to peek at her when she is getting dressed. She wants her privacy respected. He threatened to get her in trouble for something she did if she told on him.

Discussion Questions	Presenter's Response
Does Donna have the right to ask for privacy?	The privacy issue is a significant one for students grades 4 - 6.
What if Donna's brother could really get her in trouble, should she still tell?	Donna's feelings and her right to her own body are important. She could tell her parents about what she did herself, then her brother could no longer threaten her and have power over her. Telling empowers the person at risk.
What can Donna do to protect her privacy?	Don't wait for it to happen again. Tell her brother immediately. Remind her brother at the time she wants privacy so he can't claim he forgot.

Discussion Questions	Presenter's Response
What if it was her dad walking in on her, might it be harder to assert her rights?	Kids often feel they have fewer rights in relation to their parents than with siblings. Stress that it's your body. You have a right to ask your parents or anyone else for privacy. It may be hard to tell a parent but it is important.
What if it was hard to stand up to her brother? What could she do?	Discuss who she can turn to for help, or support.

Role Play: Have students take turns role playing what she can say to her brother so he really understands that this is important to her. Use this as an opportunity to teach assertive behaviors using the assertiveness techniques handout (Activity #7, Handout #2).

Role play additional situations to practice assertive behaviors. Ask students for examples of situations with their peers where they need to assert themselves. (This doesn't have to involve abuse, i.e., saying no to a friend who wants to borrow your book report.)

Scenario # 2

Your close friend, Lisa, confided to you that her mom's boyfriend, Joe, who spends a lot of time at her house (he's there practically all the time) has been making her feel very weird. He sits too close to her; he drove her to school the other day and rubbed her thigh in the car. Last night, he came into her room to say good night, and when he pulled the covers up he rubbed his hands over her body. He told her that her mom would be real angry at their special relationship, so she had better promise not to tell. Her mom was so sad when her dad left and now she is so happy since Joe's around. He also helps with money and things around the house. She decided not to tell because it would upset things too much. She made you promise not to tell anyone.

Discussion Questions	Presenter's Response
Do you think Lisa should get help with this problem?	People who do this to kids need help or restraint to stop — they can't quit on their own. If Joe is not stopped, things might get worse; this is common with sexual abuse.
What did Joe say and do to threaten Lisa not to tell? Why does he do this?	Threats and bribes are how abuse continues and how a person knows for sure that abuse is occurring. We tell kids that anytime there is a threat, bribe, or secret involved about anything, say no.

Discussion Questions	Presenter's Response
Should Lisa handle this on her own by just telling Joe no? If she does, how might she feel?	If she handles it on her own and doesn't get an adult to help her, she would remain at risk. She also would always worry that the abuse might continue and not really feel safe.
If Lisa doesn't tell and doesn't confront this problem at all, what can happen? Is it Lisa's fault if she doesn't tell?	It is likely that she would continue to be hurt and she may blame herself because the abuse continued. It is important to remember that it is never a child's fault even if you promised not to tell and even if you didn't say no. It is always wrong for a bigger and older person to trick or force a child into getting a bad touch.

Role Play: Lisa is your friend and has confided in you that this is happening and has decided not to tell. Role play encouraging your friend to get help and the reasons for doing so.

Lisa decides to tell an adult she trusts. Role play Lisa telling the presenter/teacher, who assumes the role of the person Lisa chooses to tell. The teacher/presenter responds by saying what the students need to hear to encourage telling: I believe you. It's not your fault. I'm glad you told me. It's OK to tell bad secrets and to tell even though you promised not to. I am glad you kept telling and I will help you.

Scenario # 3

Tom's coach offered to help him with some plays in the game if he stayed after practice with him alone. They practiced tackling and each time, the coach's hand ended up near or between Tom's legs. He also always seemed to end up on top of Tom and wouldn't get off right away. Last time he told Tom he was doing a great job and patted him on his bottom. Tom doesn't want to overreact or get the coach in trouble and he's not really sure if it was a coincidence or not. He's just uncomfortable about it. He's thinking about quitting the team and not saying anything. What should Tom do?

Discussion Questions	Presenter's Response
What are Tom's feelings about the coach?	It's important to trust your feelings and listen to them in order to prevent and/or stop abuse.
Why isn't he sure about what's happening?	The coach is a nice guy and usually helpful. It's confusing when someone you know, like, and trust makes you feel uncomfortable.

Discussion Questions	Presenter's Response
If Tom quits the team does that solve his problem? Why not?	This kind of problem just doesn't go away. He may feel like he did something wrong. He will be giving up the team and he didn't do anything wrong. It may affect his trust for other adults and he may not join other teams.
Could other kids be at risk too?	Yes! People who abuse children usually have many victims especially since most victims don't tell, allowing the abuse to continue.
Should Tom tell his parents?	Yes! Children need adults to help protect them. It is also very important that he hear from adults he trusts that he's not to blame, that they will help him, and that he did the right thing by telling.

Role Play: The coach has just touched Tom in a way that made him feel uncomfortable and confused. Role play Tom asserting himself with the coach.

Tom told his friend that he's thinking about quitting the team because of how the coach makes him feel. Role play Tom's friend encouraging him to get help and then going with him to an adult in school for help.

Tom turns to this parents for help. Role play Tom talking about the abuse with his parent(s). They react by being understanding, non-blaming, and supportive.

Scenario #4

Sue has a really big problem. Her dad has been sexually abusing her for two years now. It started gradually. She didn't realize or understand what was happening until things got out of hand. Sue's dad has been blaming her, saying it's her fault because she let him do it and let it go on too long. He said if she tells he'll go to jail and if she doesn't let him touch her anymore he'll just do it to her younger sister. Sue doesn't want her dad to go to jail; she just wants it to stop. She's afraid her mom will blame her, and she doesn't want her sister to be hurt. What should she do?

Discussion Questions	Presenter's Response
What is the definition of child sexual abuse?	Child sexual abuse is forced, tricked, and secret touching on private parts of your body by an older person. It usually is someone the child knows and trusts. It is the abuse of power.

Discussion Questions	Presenter's Response
Why do you think Sue didn't realize what was happening to her?	Often early stages of abuse just feel like extra attention and affection. By the time it progresses the abuser has already tricked the child to keep it a secret.
Is it Sue's fault because the abuse has been going on for two years and she was not able to stop it?	It is never ever the child's fault. The abusing adult is always responsible for the abuse.
Is Sue's younger sister safe?	No! Siblings are frequently abused at the same time without the other child knowing about it. Also, even if the father says he won't touch her sister he shouldn't be trusted since he could only stop abusing for sure with help or restraint.
Sue is worried that her mom will blame her. Do you think this could happen and why?	Sue's dad is tricking her not to tell by threatening this. It is a common threat used by abusers. If her mom isn't supportive it is because she doesn't understand about abuse and will need help as well.

Role Play: Before the role play have the class generate a list of important things for Sue's friend to tell Sue to encourage her to get help.

Then role play Sue going with her friend to the guidance counselor for help.

Activity 7 – Student Response Form

This activity develops the assertive skill of asking for help. It provides an opportunity for the students to identify grownups they could trust if they had a problem with touching or privacy. It also provides students with an opportunity to ask their teacher in private questions about the program and to ask for help if they need it.

Explain, as already discussed, how important it is to tell and get help if someone has a problem with touching or privacy and this is why students have role played going to a trusted adult for help and helping a friend get help when they need it. It is also important for each student to think about several trusted grownups if someone needs help now or at any time during the school year.

Hand out the student response form (Handout #1) with questions concerning what they learned about good and bad touches and about getting help. Read the questions one by one to the class as they complete the form.

- When you get to #3 in the Student Response Form (next page) give the students some examples of adults who can help in their school (and their names) such as yourself, another teacher they feel comfortable with, the principal, school nurse, social worker, or school psychologist.

- When you get to #4 assure the students that anyone who has questions and wants to speak with someone will have a chance to do so either later today or tomorrow. This will give you an opportunity to review the surveys, identify concerns, share them with the building principal, and notify the identified trusted adults about a student's need to speak with them.

Handout #1
Student Response Form

1. Do you think other classes should have a program about good and bad touches in school?
   - ❑ yes
   - ❑ no

2. Check what you learned during the program:
   - ❑ I learned about saying no to touches that make me feel bad or uncomfortable.
   - ❑ I learned about telling if I need help.
   - ❑ I learned about who to tell if I get a bad touch.

3. Name three grownups you trust to talk to if you had a problem about touching or privacy. If possible include an adult in school, an adult family member or relative, and an adult friend or an adult in the community that you trust.

   _____

   _____

   _____

4. Do you have any questions about the program you would like to ask your teacher privately?
   - ❑ yes
   - ❑ no

5. Do you or someone you know need help with a problem about bad touches?
   - ❑ yes
   - ❑ no

If you answered yes, who would you like to talk to in your school about it?

_____

_____
Student's name

Handout # 2 – Assertiveness Techniques

Assertive Body Language:

■ Body Posture: Stand straight and tall.

■ Facial expression: Look serious and do not smile.

■ Eye contact: Look directly at the person to whom you are speaking.

Verbal Assertive Skills:

■ Say no: Actually say the word "no" rather than using weaker phrases such as "I don't think so."

■ Use your important voice: The way you say no or the way you refuse makes a difference in whether you are taken seriously. Use a strong voice to be believed.

■ Don't give excuses: Tell the person exactly how you feel.

■ Say no over and over again: Keep saying no until the person listens to you and believes you really mean it.

■ Use "I" Statements: Say "I want" you to stop what your doing.

Unit 2: Teasing, Bullying, and Sexual Harassment Prevention

Part A: Resource Materials for Educators

Note to Presenters

Teasing, bullying, and disrespectful behavior is a regular part of going to school for many students. It is often thought of as a rite of passage and just part of growing up. This expectation fosters acceptance of a standard of behavior that is reinforced just by its existence. Because kids are expected to be mean to each other, they are mean to each other. When kids feel the only response available when dealing with teasing and bullying is to ignore it and just put up with it, they are bound to feel helpless and without options. The myth that taking action will only make things worse becomes a reality when the adults who are supposed to protect kids buy into this same myth. Telling kids to stand up for themselves without consistent adult responses or rules that define acceptable behavior is ineffective. If kids have to continue to go it alone nothing will change and the culture will continue to allow disrespectful behaviors to flourish.

A personal anecdote strongly emphasizes this point:

I moved to a new community when my son was seven and in third grade. The kids in his class had grown up together and greeted him as an outsider. He was teased and left out simply because he was "the new kid on the block." After a while he started to come home with stories about being left out of this game and that game during recess, how the kids started to tease him, and that it was only getting worse.

I called his teacher and alerted her to the problem, she thanked me and said she would take care of it. What I didn't know was that she told my son that he had to "learn to stand up for himself and that she couldn't come out in front of the class and say something because that would be tattling and it would only get worse." Since my initial efforts did not work and his teacher was ineffective, my son began to suffer in silence.

One day his teacher got the flu and a young substitute teacher was temporarily in charge. On this new teacher's first day, once again during recess my son was left out. Right after recess the class had a chance to write in their journals. My son wrote about how bad he felt about the way he was being treated. The substitute teacher read his words and immediately addressed the class. They were told that this would be the last time anyone would be left out of anything during recess and teased — or else. My son's problem ended right there. The other kid's mean behavior stopped as soon as an adult took responsibility to make sure that it did.

Part A: Resource Materials for Educators

The materials presented in this unit help children — and the adults who protect them — build a positive school community and create a climate where disrespectful behavior is not accepted. The activities can be used to prevent sexual harassment on the elementary school level, peer bullying and teasing, and discriminatory behavior based on gender, race, ethnic background, and disabilities. Unlike other educational resources on bullying and teasing, this manual not only addresses peer behaviors but the behavior rules developed apply to the adults as well. Therefore, it can be used to prevent student-to-student harassment and adult-to-student sexual harassment as well as child sexual abuse in the school environment. The emphasis is on promoting self-respect and respectful treatment of children and adults alike.

In addition, please note that the materials in Unit 2 are based on and expand upon the concepts of child sexual abuse prevention found in Unit 1 of this teaching guide. The main focus is on teaching children that they deserve good treatment at home and in school from their peers and adults — and it is the adults who will ensure that children's rights are protected. Therefore, the activities in Unit 2B provide an ideal opportunity to effectively reinforce the child sexual abuse prevention skills already taught in the classroom.

Teaching Guidelines

Sexual harassment in the schools is widely being recognized as a major problem. A recent study by the American Association of University Women (AAUW) found that 39 percent of girls reported being harassed at school on a daily basis during their last school year, that 75 percent of sexual harassment was between students and 4 percent was by teachers, administrators, and other school staff. The most common forms of harassment students reported were sexual comments, gestures, looks, teasing, and jokes. These subtle and overt forms of sexually aggressive behaviors are part of the continuum of violence. Sex-based teasing and bullying in the younger grades becomes harassment later on and milder forms of harassment can become assaultive. By addressing the milder disrespectful behaviors, the escalation of hurtful behaviors can be prevented and the right of all students to be safe and receive good treatment is validated.

A great deal of media attention has focused on sexual harassment between students on the elementary school level. School officials are depicted as over-reacting for suspending young students with minor infractions out of fear of liability. As a result the labeling of young children's inappropriate behavior as sexual harassment is being questioned. Nevertheless, there have been serious cases of sexual harassment against children as young as six years old and the law does apply and is actionable on the elementary school level.

While it is necessary to implement a prevention program for elementary school children, it is recommended that when teaching children appropriate behavior in grades K-6, the term sexual harassment not be used unless the behavior in question is specifically gender based or sexual in nature. Instead, the main focus should be on teaching children that they are entitled to respectful, humane treatment both at home and in school from their peers and adults. The emphasis should be on promoting self-respect and respectful treatment of others in the school environment. Children need to be taught school behavior rules that protect students and the rights to their own body so that school is a safe and positive place.

The educator's resource material included in this section provides an understanding of sexual harassment, the law, and guidelines for developing school policies and procedures. It includes the components of a comprehensive program for promoting a respectful school environment and information about the educator's role in addressing peer harassment, bullying, and teasing.

Administrators: Prior to implementing the teasing, bullying, and sexual harassment prevention program

- Make sure that all professional and non-professional staff have had training in the use of the school's sexual harassment policy.

- Review the sexual harassment grievance and reporting procedures developed by your district with the building support staff whose responsibility it may be to follow up with student concerns.

- Review the procedures in-place for handling mandated reporting of child abuse with the teaching staff.

- Consider a letter to parents that includes a statement explaining that schools are required under Title IX of the Equal Employment Opportunity Commission (EEOC) federal guidelines to develop a sexual harassment policy and provide training for all students and staff. By doing so the school district meets its legal requirements and more importantly, helps create an environment that is safe, healthy, and provides educational opportunities for all students. Emphasize that on the elementary school level the focus will be not on sexual harassment per se but on promoting respectful behavior.

Teachers/Presenters: Prior to implementing the program:

- Review Unit 2A paying special attention to the material entitle Educator's Role in Addressing Peer Sexual Harassment, Bullying, and Teasing. These are guidelines to help educators respond effectively when a student comes to an adult with a concern and when an adult witnesses disrespectful behavior.

- Review Unit 1A which contains information on handling student disclosures, mandated reporting, indicators of child abuse and maltreatment, and recognizing the academic and emotional clues of child abuse in the classroom.

- Review your school's procedures on handling disclosures of child abuse and neglect.

- Alert the building principal if there are concerns about any student's participation in the program.

- Inform support personnel when you will be teaching the sexual harassment prevention program so that they will be prepared in the event a child discloses and needs further assistance.

Following the presentation all teachers should:

- Reinforce with the students the availability for help if needed.

- Share any concerns about student(s) resulting from the program with the building principal.

- Reinforce throughout the school year everyone's right to their own bodies and respectful treatment by their peers and the adults who work in school.

Sexual Harassment*

Preventing Sexual Harassment

In 1992 the U.S. Supreme Court ruled in the *Franklin v. Gwinnett County* school district case that victims of sexual harassment and sex discrimination in schools may sue their school districts for monetary damages. This case involved a female student who alleged that she reported to school officials on many occasions that a male teacher was sexually harassing her, and that school officials did nothing to stop the harassment and attempted to convince her not to file a formal complaint. This decision has lead many school districts to seek help in developing sexual harassment prevention programs.

Under Title IX sexual harassment is defined as unwelcome sexual advances, requests for sexual favors, and other verbal or physical conduct of a sexual nature.

- It is illegal when Someone in position of authority, such as a teacher, requires a student to submit to sexually harassing behavior as a condition of a grade, or as a condition of acceptance or continuation in any educational or extracurricular activity;

- It is illegal when unwelcome sexual behavior by a student, teacher, administrator, or other school personnel creates an intimidating, hostile, or offensive environment or unreasonably interferes with a person's school performance or education.

Simply having a sexual harassment policy is not enough to reduce liability. Because school districts are responsible for the actions of their employees, they may be liable under Title IX whether or not the school was aware of the harassment and even if it had a policy prohibiting sexual harassment. The key factor in determining liability is whether or not a school fails to take corrective action or whether the remedial action it does take is appropriate. When schools respond appropriately to sexual harassment concerns, they can prevent the school environment from continuing to be hostile and from interfering with the student's performance or education, thereby satisfying their legal responsibility.

The most effective way to reduce legal liability is by establishing sexual harassment policies, developing procedures for handling complaints, and training students and staff in the prevention of sexual harassment. The best reason to implement prevention training programs is ultimately to end harassment, not merely to avoid liability. It is essential that students are enabled to pursue their education freely, cooperate and learn from each other, and contribute to their schools and community. When schools cultivate an environment that is safe, healthy, and affords positive educational opportunities for all students, it enhances the morale of the entire school, the confidence and self-respect of its individual students and school personnel.

The following checklist can help educators determine if they have taken the necessary steps towards preventing sexual harassment in their own school environment.

✓ Does your school have a firm sexual harassment policy that is easy to understand and widely distributed?

✓ Have *both* faculty and students received sexual harassment training in the implementation of the policy and the procedures for handling complaints?

✓ Are students informed about ways to avoid harassment and defend their rights?

✓ Does your school take effective action when informed of specific occurrences of sexual harassment?

✓ Has a sexual harassment prevention program been implemented for *both* faculty and students encouraging their awareness and understanding of the problem and their involvement in its prevention?

Implementing a Proactive Rather than Reactive Prevention Approach

Set standards for acceptable student behavior. This provides an opportunity to react to behavior in the halls and classrooms as disrespectful and not permitted, rather than labeling all behaviors as sexual harassment. Letting students know "we have rules against that behavior here and that's not allowed or appropriate" takes the emphasis off "harassment" *per se* and puts it back on teaching students to consider the feelings of others and on taking responsibility for their own behavior.

Inform all staff of their responsibility for imposing the rules regarding acceptable student behavior. Including all staff in the scope of authority is particularly crucial because adult silences are seen by young people as negligence that allows harassment and disrespectful behaviors to continue. The loss of trust that comes from inaction on the part of adults can also extend to witnesses of the harassment, boys as well as girls.

Encourage students to be positive role models. Students need to learn *how* to behave differently and *how* to react differently to unacceptable behaviors through the modeling of positive behaviors. Use and create teachable moments to talk openly about which behaviors are not OK. The goal here is for both male and females not to be afraid to confront behaviors that are unacceptable. Students should be encouraged by teachers to speak up and support their friends when their friends are targets of disrespectful behavior. They should also receive positive reinforcement when they bring concerns to adults about a friend's or their own need for help.

Emphasize the importance for all teachers, administrators, and adults working in the school environment to behave as positive role models for students. Teachers, in particular, should behave toward students in a respectful manner and expect respectful treatment from other adults and students in school. In all areas of student life (academic and extracurricular) the importance of valuing all kinds of people and their differences based on gender, culture, ethnic, and racial background should be emphasized. Educators should talk openly about all people deserving good treatment using examples from students own experiences and the media.

Developing a Sexual Harassment Policy*

Your policy should clearly state that sexual harassment will not be tolerated in your school. You should define sexual harassment and the sanctions against it, explain the procedures for filing a complaint, and explain how the complaint will be handled. You should also explain how your sexual harassment policy and procedures coordinate with other disciplinary procedures existing within your school. The following are some guidelines for writing a sexual harassment policy.

The Process of Adopting a Policy

When writing a sexual harassment policy, include representatives from all the constituencies in your school such as teachers, staff members, and students if possible. This serves two purposes. First, the policy will be better if it takes into account the viewpoints of everyone affected by it. Second, the process of adopting a policy can serve as an educating experience for community members and will increase their involvement and commitment to ending sexual harassment.

Prohibition of Sexual Harassment

The policy should contain a clear and forceful statement by the school superintendent and/or top administrators that harassment is prohibited and will not be tolerated. Explain that sexual harassment is a problem that negatively affects both individual students and the community as a whole.

Definition of Sexual Harassment

The policy should concisely describe prohibited behavior and include specific examples. It should cover both subtle and blatant behavior. Let the students know that their actions may be sexual harassment, not just the actions of

---

*Reprinted with permission from *Policies and Procedures on Sexual Harassment in Schools: A Guide for Administrators.* New York: NOW Legal Defense and Education Fund, 1995.

teachers. Let teachers know that they have a responsibility to supervise students and report sexual harassment.

Complaint Procedures

Your policy should clearly explain how to file a complaint, how the complaint will be handled, and how long the process will take. You should try to avoid face to face confrontations, which may be traumatic for a target of harassment.

The policy should designate several people who will receive complaints and give their names, office locations, and telephone numbers. Ideally the policy should supply both district and local level complaint receivers. Those designated to receive complaints should be specially trained. However, all teachers and staff need to know how to respond if a student comes to them with a complaint or if they witness harassment.

You should provide both formal and informal complaint procedures. Both types of complaints should be investigated. A formal complaint process should include an investigation, a grievance procedure, a written report, and an opportunity to appeal.

On the other hand, if a student wants to make an informal complaint, the complaint receiver should assist the student in communicating with the harasser and requesting the harassment to stop. This option will encourage some students who might hesitate in making a formal claim to feel comfortable reporting their problems. An informal complaint will also give you the opportunity to deal with the situation before it gets too bad. Interim relief procedures should also be offered.

These complaint procedures may operate in conjunction with general sex discrimination grievance procedures required by Title IX. Include a time line for each step of the complaint, investigation, grievance, resolution, and appeal. Note that internal school complaint mechanisms cannot lawfully forestall a target of harassment from pursuing complaint procedures with local, state, and federal agencies.

Sanctions

The policy should detail what sanctions will apply for engaging in prohibited activity. You should impose a range of penalties, including suspension and expulsion, and tie the penalties to the severity of the harassment and the perpetrator's prior history. Distinguish between sanctions for the student harasser, the adult harasser, and the adult who is aware of sexual harassment but fails to act in accordance with school policy and procedures. Sanctions should be commensurate with school discipline in other contexts. In some cases, you may need to reassign or suspend (with pay) an employee pending an investigation or disciplinary action in accord with your other disciplinary policies.

Confidentiality

Confidential investigations are critical to protect everyone involved. For example, lack of confidentiality may lead to the harassed student becoming unfairly labeled a "troublemaker," and as a result, experiencing more harassment and stress. Lack of confidentiality may also lead to damaged careers or reputations and may undermine confidence and trust in the school's administration. All written and oral communications about a complaint should be confidential. Information should be disclosed only on a need-to-know basis and with the understanding that the recipient has a duty to preserve confidentiality.

Protection Against Retaliation

Students will not be comfortable coming forward unless they are confident they will be treated fairly and not further harmed. The policy must stress the complainants will not face repercussions and that anyone who takes any action in retaliation for the filing of a complaint will face the same range of sanctions as the original harasser.

Investigations

The policy should provide for a neutral and well-trained investigator to follow-up on complaints. It is optimal for there to be a female investigator and a female receiver of complaints available because sometimes female students feel uncomfortable talking to male investigators or complaint handlers. Ask your students to recommend people they trust and respect. The investigation should be prompt, thorough, and impartial.

Policy Distribution

The policy must reach every member of the community. Use your customary means of distribution, including posting the policy on bulletin boards, reviewing it with students and staff at the beginning of each academic year, and including it in employee and student handbooks or with employee paychecks. You may require each employee to actually sign off that they received and read the policy. Finally, you should inform parents about the sexual harassment policy and procedures.

Education and Training

All students, teachers, and staff should participate in education and training on sexual harassment. As a preventive measure, these programs should acquaint everyone with the school's sexual harassment policy and procedures and demonstrate how they are applied to real-life situations. You should also design special programs for those who violate the policy.

Support Services

The policy should include information on individuals such as nurses, counselors, psychologists, and social workers who are available to help students determine if they have been harassed and cope with the effects of harassment. You may also want to establish peer support groups for students.

Mechanisms for Feedback

You should develop mechanisms to review the policy, procedures, and programs at your school as well as evaluate the sensitivity of those handling and investigating complaints on an annual basis. Also, you should develop ways to "check" the atmosphere around the school, such as setting up task forces or conducting periodic surveys.

About Sexual Harassment*

What is sexual harassment?

Sexual harassment is unwelcome sexual comments, gestures, jokes, looks, behavior, requests for sex, rumors, being touched in a sexual way, or being forced to do something sexual. Sexual harassment is against the law at work and at school. In schools, it is illegal for a teacher or any school employee to sexually harass a student or another school employee and for a student to harass a teacher, a school employee, or another student. The most common kind of sexual harassment in schools is student-to-student harassment and it usually happens in public. Both male and female students report being victims of harassment.

What is meant by unwelcome?

Whether or not behavior is unwelcome depends upon how an individual person feels about the way the other person is behaving. Two people may experience the same behavior differently. One may take it as a compliment or may not feel offended by it, and the other may not want to be treated that way or may feel uncomfortable about it.

Can a person be accused of sexual harassment even if the person did not intend to harass anyone?

Yes. Someone may intend to harmlessly tease, joke, or flirt with the other person and not realize how they are making the other person feel. If you do not want to harass another person then you need to think about how your actions will be received and the effect they may have on the other person. It helps to understand the difference between flirting and harassment:

Flirting: wanted • welcome • returned • feels good • compliment • legal

Harassment: unwanted • unwelcome • unreturned • feels bad • put-down • illegal

If a person does not say no or object to your behavior is this still harassment?

Yes. A person may be too embarrassed, uncomfortable or afraid to speak up. Often the first reaction is to try to ignore the behavior and act like it doesn't bother you especially if you are outnumbered by a group of people. The person being harassed is hoping the behavior will stop if they don't say anything and may think it will only get worse if they do react. Actually it only gets worse if it's ignored because the students who are doing the harassing may think their behavior is OK. It's usually confusing for everyone involved.

How can someone know if their behavior is sexual harassment if they are not told their behavior is unwelcome?

If the answer is no to two or more of the following questions, there is a good chance the behavior is unwelcome. Would I say or do the same to someone of the same sex? Would I say or do this if my parent, girlfriend, boyfriend, or teacher were present? Would I want someone else to say or do this to my sister, brother, girlfriend, or boyfriend? Is the person to whom I'm saying or doing this in an equal position of power as me? Do my words or actions show respect for the other person?

Is it sexual harassment if the behavior is not directed toward you but you observe it and find it offensive and unwelcome?

Yes. Regardless of whether the person experiencing the behavior finds it unwelcome or not, it is sexual harassment if it creates a negative school environment for others.

Sexual Harassment Policy for Secondary School Students*

Sexual harassment is against the law. The board of education prohibits sexual harassment by a student, teacher, administrator, or by any adult who works or volunteers in the school district.

Definition of Sexual Harassment

Sexual harassment is unwelcome verbal sexual advances, requests for sexual favors, or other verbal or physical conduct of a sexual nature. Some examples of sexual harassment experienced in school that may be grounds for complaint are:

- comments, jokes, innuendos, gestures or looks of a sexual or lewd nature
- references to gender, or name calling
- unwelcome touching, grabbing, or pinching
- flashing or mooning
- sexually offensive pictures, graffiti
- being intentionally brushed up against or blocked
- having clothing pulled
- being forced to kiss someone or do something sexual other than kissing
- sexual rumors or requests for sexual favors
- being spied on while dressing or showering

Sexual Harassment Is Illegal

- It is illegal when unwelcome sexual behavior by a student, teacher, administrator, or other school personnel creates an intimidating, hostile, or offensive environment or interferes with a student's school performance or education.

- It is illegal when someone in a position of authority, such as a teacher, requires a student to submit to sexually harassing behavior as a condition of a grade, or as a condition of acceptance or continuation in any educational or extracurricular activity.

If You Are Sexually Harassed

- You are not to blame for what happened to you.
- Don't ignore the problem, it may only get worse.
- It is your right to go to school in a safe and comfortable environment.
- Take action to protect those rights.

How to Report Sexual Harassment

In an incident involving another student that is not a serious concern, talk to any trusted adult in school who can support your resolve by:

- helping you decide what actions to take;
- helping you tell the other student that his or her behavior bothers you and that you want it to stop;
- informing the person for you about his or her unwanted behavior;
- helping you file a complaint if you are unable to reach resolution.

Report a serious complaint immediately to any trusted adult. It may involve a student, teacher, or any other adult as the harasser. A serious complaint is when:

- the harassing behavior has been going on for some time;
- it involves physical or sexual assault, threats, or intimidation;
- the person has refused to stop or change the harassing behavior when confronted.

Remember: Sexual harassment is prohibited and illegal! Appropriate discipline ranging from a reprimand up to and including suspension or expulsion will be imposed upon any student or adult

■ found to sexually harass any person in the school environment;

■ found to retaliate against anyone who reports a sexual harassment complaint;

■ found to make false charges of sexual harassment against a student or adult.

The Educator's Role in Addressing Peer Sexual Harassment, Bullying, and Teasing

When a Student Comes to an Adult with a Concern

Students are encouraged to express their concerns to any trusted adult in the school. The following are overall guidelines to help educators respond effectively. They apply any time a student comes to an adult for help regardless of whether the concern is mild, moderate, or serious.

Always take any concern and students' feelings seriously. It is important not to minimize, condone, or treat disrespectful behavior lightly. This can be accomplished by telling the student:

■ He or she did the right thing by coming to see you.

■ Every student has a right to tell and get help if they are having a problem with how they are being treated in school.

■ Telling to get help is not tattling.

Communicate to the student that it was not his or her fault.

Determine how serious the problem is for the student.

■ Clarify how often they have been treated this way, how long has this been happening, and if the student knows if its happening to anyone else.

■ If this is the first time the behavior has occurred, let the student know they are doing the right thing by wanting the behavior to stop and not waiting to see if it happens again. They are helping to protect themselves and other students as well.

Reinforce the student's right not to ignore the problem or have to handle it alone.

■ Ask the student how they have responded so far to the problem. Make sure the student understands that anything he or she has tried to do to protect him or herself is OK including avoiding the person or running away.

■ If the concern is not serious in nature and doesn't involve a physical or sexual assault, ask the student how they would be comfortable handling the situation. Offer to figure it out together and continue helping the student until the problem is solved.

- If the student making the disclosure doesn't want the other student(s) to know who told but wants the disrespectful behavior to stop, suggest that you will watch out for a recurrence of the behavior, confront it when you see it, make sure that the behavior stops, and the student is safe.

Follow-up to make sure there is no reoccurrence or retaliation.

- Emphasize the student's right to go to school in a safe and positive environment and that you will check to make sure the bullying or teasing has stopped.
- The student should be encouraged to let the adult know if it happens again or if someone says you had better not tell or else.
- Stress that the student(s) who did the teasing or bullying will be watched to make sure they do not tease or bully anyone else.

Inform the building principal. Anytime the complaint involves physical or sexual assault the principal should be informed immediately.

If the concern involves behavior outside the classroom such as on the bus, in the lunchroom, or during recess the building principal should be made aware of the situation. The principal can then determine, based on other complaints, whether this is a pattern and serious in nature and whether it warrants additional adult supervision.

It is also necessary that the building principal be informed whenever the disclosure involves sexual or gender-based teasing or bullying. You will be following your school's sexual harassment policy by doing so.

When an Adult Witnesses Disrespectful Behavior

All teachers, support staff, and administrators need to know how to address bullying, teasing, and sexual harassment when they see it. If behaviors are not consistently addressed it is impossible to effect a positive change in the culture of a school environment. Liability becomes an issue for a school district when educators fail to respond or do not respond appropriately to sexual harassment when they witness it. Some examples of behaviors that may constitute sexual harassment on the elementary school level include: calling a boy "gay," "sissy," or a "girl"; calling a girl a "bitch," a "slut," a "tomboy" or "boy"; unwelcome touching; grabbing, pinching, touching of private parts; pulling girls' skirts up, having other clothing pulled at; pulling down boys' pants; sexual comments, rumors, pictures, graffiti or notes; being forced to do something sexual. The section that follows, Guidelines for Handling Sexual or Gender-Based Teasing or Bullying, expands upon how to handle sexual harassment on the elementary school level.

Directly confront inappropriate behavior when you observe it. Ignoring disrespectful behavior only reinforces it. It is also ineffective to stop the behavior by saying cut it out or go back to class without taking the following further actions:

- Immediately tell the student who is acting inappropriately that the behavior is not allowed and against the school behavior rules. On the elementary school level it is recommended not to refer to behavior specifically as sexual harassment but rather as disrespectful.

- If you are not the student's teacher let the student know that their teacher will be told and handling this concern. Depending on the severity of the behavior, the classroom teacher may need to refer the matter to the building principal.

- Do not overreact in front of the targeted student. This can be embarrassing and upsetting. Instead take the misbehaving student(s) aside as soon as it's practical.

- Ask the student(s) to make a commitment to stop the behavior.

- With a first-time offense and if the behavior is not serious, let the student know disciplinary action will be taken if it happens again.

- Let the student know you will be watching him or her to make sure the behavior doesn't continue and will be checking with the targeted student to make sure the behavior has stopped.

- If this is not a first-time offense follow through with appropriate consequences according to school procedures.

Assess the extent and nature of the problem

- When a group of students behaves in a disrespectful manner towards one or more students it is important to determine the seriousness of the behavior witnessed. You will need to know if this is an isolated incident, a pattern of behavior, how long it has been going on, and how pervasive it is.

- Discuss the behavior with other teachers and administrators to provide clarification and encourage other adults to make a proactive response when observing similar behavior.

Support the targeted student

- When you observe one or more students being disrespectful to another student it is not necessary or appropriate to ask publicly if the targeted student wants to report it.

- The adult who witnesses the behavior has the responsibility to address and/or report it.

- To enable educators to respond effectively and help the targeted student, review the guidelines outlined in the preceding section, the Educator's Role in Addressing Peer Sexual Harassment, Bullying, and Teasing.

Guidelines for Handling Sexual or
Gender-Based Teasing and Bullying*

The Office of Civil Rights issued a document, "Sexual Harassment Guidance," to help schools appropriately address allegations of student sexual harassment. The following is a summary of information contained in this document which provides important clarification for elementary school educators:

- Title IX of the Education Amendments of 1972 (Title IX) prohibits discrimination on the basis of sex in education programs and activities receiving federal financial assistance. Sexual harassment of students is a form of discrimination prohibited by Title IX.

- Sexual harassment is prohibited under Title IX for all the academic, educational, extra-curricular, athletic, and other programs of the school, whether they take place within the school's facilities, on the bus, in a classroom, or training program sponsored by the school at another location, or elsewhere.

- All school employees are obligated to let the school official (building principal) know whenever they have knowledge of teasing or bullying that is gender based or sexual in nature. The law requires that if the behavior is assessed to be part of a pattern, severe, persistent, or pervasive in creating a hostile environment a school must take immediate and appropriate steps to stop it and prevent its reoccurrence.

- Age is relevant in determining whether sexual harassment occurred in the first instance, as well as determining the appropriate response by the school. For example a kiss on the cheek by a first grader does not constitute sexual harassment.

- School employees or officials may rely entirely on their own judgment regarding how best to handle inappropriate conduct that does not rise to the level of harassment prohibited by Title IX.

- Title IX permits the use of a general student disciplinary procedure. The discipline should be age appropriate and follow an escalating range of consequences based on the severity of the behavior. The critical issue is whether responsive action taken is effective in ending the sexual harassment and preventing its reoccurrence.

- Title IX's prohibition of sexual harassment does not extend to legitimate nonsexual touching or other nonsexual conduct. For example a kindergarten teacher's consoling hug for a child with a skinned knee will not be considered sexual harassment. However, a teacher's repeated hugging and putting his or her arm around students under inappropriate circumstances could create a hostile environment.

---

*Adapted from Office of Civil Rights, "Sexual Harassment Guidance: Harassment of Students by School Employees, Other Students, or Third Parties." Washington, D.C.: *Federal Register,* 1997 (Vol. 62, No. 49).

- Both male and female students are protected from sexual harassment engaged in by a school's employees, other students, or third parties regardless of the sex of the harasser, for example, sexually explicit graffiti directed at a particular girl by other girls.

- A school will always be liable for even one instance of harassment by a school employee in a position of authority, such as a teacher or administrator, whether or not school personnel knew or should have known. A school will also be liable for creating a hostile environment through sexual harassment by its employees. In some cases the younger the student is, the more likely it is that he or she will consider any adult employee to be in position of authority including cafeteria workers and aids.

- In contrast to a school's liability for sexual harassment by its employees, Title IX does not make a school responsible for the actions of harassing students but rather for its own discrimination in failing to remedy it once the school has notice. Upon notice of hostile-environment harassment, a school must take immediate and appropriate steps to remedy the hostile environment in order to avoid violating Title IX.

- Schools are required to adopt and publish grievance procedures that provide for discovering sexual harassment as early as possible and for effectively correcting problems.

- In the absence of effective policies and grievance procedures a school will be in violation of Title IX when a hostile environment exists, even if the school was not aware of the harassment and thus failed to remedy it.

- In order to be actionable as harassment, sexual conduct must be unwelcome. Conduct is considered unwelcome if the student did not request or invite it and "regarded the conduct as undesirable or offensive." When younger children are involved, the age of the student will be considered, the nature of the conduct involved, and other relevant factors in determining whether a student had the capacity to welcome sexual conduct from other students. Sexual conduct between an adult school employee and any elementary or secondary school student will never be viewed as consensual.

Components of a Comprehensive Prevention Program for Promoting a Respectful School Environment

Through the implementation of comprehensive prevention programs, many school districts are making efforts to address the milder disrespectful behaviors that can lead to assault. This proactive rather than a reactive response incorporates training for teachers, staff, administrators, and the student body in the prevention of both sexual harassment and disrespectful behavior on all grade levels, K-12. It is important that administrators remain involved throughout the program's planning and implementation in order to demonstrate a commitment to zero tolerance and for schools to incorporate the following steps:

1. Evaluate the School Climate. In order to plan a program addressing the specific needs of a school it is necessary to assess whether there are existing concerns that require attention by seeking input from both students and staff. The following efforts enable this process:

Discussions and/or questionnaires with educators and nonprofessional staff that covers:

- What kinds of teasing and/or bullying behaviors are present (either witnessed or reported) in this school environment?
- Are there certain areas in the school where these concerns are more prevalent?
- Are there particular students, groups of students, particular classes, or grade levels that have problems with being disrespectful?
- Do students bring their concerns to adults for help with teasing or bullying by peers?
- Do students bring their concerns to adults for help with when the concern involves another adult in school?
- How have adults responded when they've seen disrespectful behavior thus far?
- What do students do when they witness teasing and bullying?
- How do the nonteaching staff handle teasing and bullying when they see it?

An organized plan for obtaining information about students' experiences through the students' own eyes. Students can begin to take ownership of the problem and adults can get a better picture of how effective their efforts have been to be helpful to students through:

- **School-Wide Student Survey.** This tends to give an over-all picture of the problem and can serve as an impetus to jump start a comprehensive prevention program.
- **Classroom Student Discussions about What's Happening.** This approach effectively gives students a chance to be more specific about their concerns, problem solve ways to help each other when they witness teasing and bullying, and discuss how to prevent it in the first place. Peer Power and the How Kids See It handout (Activity #9 in Part 2B) are classroom activities intended for this purpose.

2. Set a Standard of Respectful Behavior. Faculty, administrators, and other school personnel should serve as role models of respectful behavior to encourage students to behave respectfully in school. In addition, respectful behavior is more likely to become the standard of behavior by establishing the following:

School Behavior Rules (Unit 2B, Activity #7, Handout #1). This should apply to appropriate behavior for students and adults alike.

Class Bill of Rights (Unit 2B, Activity #5 for K–3 and Activity #12 for 4–6). If each classroom practices zero tolerance for disrespectful behavior and supports individual students' rights it can result in a positive effect on the school climate as a whole.

Consequences for Violation of School Behavior Rules. These consequences should escalate according to the severity of behavior, age appropriateness, and to help students change inappropriate behavior.

Clear Guidelines for Handling the Violation of Rules. Adults need clear guidelines in order to be consistent in their response to disrespectful behavior. When students see a consistent response by adults they feel protected.

Follow-up Procedures. The only way to ensure the continued safety of students is to follow-up with the targeted student and make sure the behavior has not reoccurred, and there has been no retaliation.

3. **Provide Faculty and Staff Training**

    Sexual harassment prevention training should include
    *   an overview of the problem, the law, and ways to reduce liability
    *   training in the use of the school district's sexual harassment policy
    *   faculty's role in implementing policy, responding to incidents, and in preventing harassment of adult and peer harassment
    *   staff's role for reporting incidents of adult and peer harassment
    *   training in the use of curriculum materials that promotes respectful treatment in the school environment

    Intensive training for administrators and support staff in effective handling of disclosures
    *   establishing investigation procedures
    *   helping students cope with the effects of harassment and dealing with the aftermath
    *   developing procedures for handling mandated reporting
    *   establishing follow-up procedures, training, and prevention programs

    In child abuse prevention training, it is important to include
    *   a review of the following since child abuse disclosures can result during the teaching of sexual harassment prevention.
    *   an overview of the problem: facts, indicators, and prevalence
    *   educators' role as mandated reporters and reporting to child protective services

- school procedures in place for handling disclosures

4. Develop Programs that Reinforce a Positive School Climate

Faculty/Parent Task Force. This group can be responsible for evaluating the programs in place, for encouraging school and community support for on-going programs, and for planning future programs.

Peer leadership Programs. Train groups of students to mediate, resolve conflicts, report concerns, and be buddies to younger students.

Social Skills Student Development. Encourage classroom instruction that teaches conflict resolution, assertiveness training, promoting self-esteem, diversity acceptance, empathy, and effective communication skills.

Student Task Force. This is a student group that runs programs to further promote a respectful school environment such as a poster contest about bullying, or puppet shows and skits for younger grades about how to handle teasing and bullying. The students can also problem solve about areas of concern.

Resources

Educator's Resources

Fink, Marjorie. *Adolescent Sexual Assault and Prevention Curriculum.* Holmes Beach, Fla.: Learning Publications, 1995. This comprehensive manual includes resources and curriculum materials for educators to use in the classroom that emphasize teaching prevention strategies that empower adolescents with both the knowledge and skills needed to help them protect their own bodies, their rights and the rights of others. It covers the prevention of sexual harassment in schools, child sexual abuse, date and acquaintance rape, sexual exploitation, dating violence, and campus rape.

Hostile Hallways: The AAUW Survey on Sexual Harassment in America's Schools. Washington, D.C.: American Association of University Women, 1993. Results of a survey on boys and girls indicating the extent of sexual harassment in American schools.

Layman, Nancy S. *Sexual Harassment in American Secondary Schools: A Legal Guide for Administrators, Teachers, and Students.* Dallas: Contemporary Research Press, 1994. This resource thoroughly covers the law, guidelines for school behavior, procedures to reduce harassment, how to create a policy, and develop and implement informal and formal grievance procedures.

Olweus, Dan. *Bullying at School: What We Know and What We Can Do About It.* Cambridge, Mass.: Blackwell Publishing, 1993. Discusses a program for Norwegian schools which is the first bullying prevention program based on scientific research. Covers the prevalence of bullying and its effect on students.

Policies and Procedures on Sexual Harassment in Schools: Guide for Administrators. New York: NOW Legal Defense and Education Fund, 1995. Excellent resource for developing a model policy on sexual harassment in the schools.

"School Safety: Bully-Free Schools," *National School Safety Center News Journal.* Malibu: Pepperdine University's National School Safety Center, Fall 1996. This entire issue is dedicated to bullying prevention in the schools and contains a number of articles about school-based programs and a sample student survey on bullying in school.

"Sexual Harassment Guidance: Harassment of Students by School Employees, Other Students, or Third Parties." Washington, D.C.: Office of Civil Rights, *Federal Register,* March 13, 1997 (Vol. 62, No. 49). This guide provides education institutions with information regarding the standards used by the Office for Civil Rights (OCR), as a model for institutions to investigate and resolve sexual harassment allegations.

Shoop, Robert J., and Jack W. Hayhow Jr. *Sexual Harassment in Our Schools: What Parents and Teachers Need to Know to Spot It and Stop It.* Mass.: Allyn, 1994. This manual covers the causes, consequences, the law, and information on developing sexual harassment policies and procedures in school. Also contains thorough lists of Gender Equity Resources.

Stein, Nan. *Secrets in Public: Sexual Harassment in Public (and Private) Schools.* Working paper #256. Wellesley, Mass.: Wellesley College Center for Research on Women, 1993. A resource demonstrating student-to-student and teacher-to-student harassment.

Webb, Susan L. *Step Forward: Sexual Harassment in the Workplace. What You Need to Know!* New York: Multimedia, 1991. A clear, concise, practical book on sexual harassment in the workplace. It covers developing policy and procedures, handling complaints, and how to prevent harassment in the work environment.

Sexual Harassment, Teasing, and Bullying Prevention Videos

Big Changes, Big Choices: Respecting Others. The Bureau for At-Risk Youth, 645 New York Ave., Huntington, NY 11743. VHS 1/2" cassette, 30 minutes. (800) 99-YOUTH. This video, featuring comedian/youth counselor Michael Pritchard talking to groups of students, teaches young adolescents the notion that everybody deserves respect, that they need to become aware of the many ways in which they show both respect and disrespect toward each other, and learn to appreciate differences in others rather than fear them. Suggested for grade levels 5-9.

Bullies: Violence Cessation. World Educational Media, Plainview, N.Y.: The Bureau For At-Risk Youth. 1-800-99-YOUTH. Bullying can be the first introduction the elementary student has to a life of violence. Successfully tested on students, this video-based curriculum puts a stop to the potential violence-forming lifestyle of Bullying. Includes a teacher's guide and student evaluation forms. Suggested for grades 1-5.

Don't Pick on Me. Sunburst Communications, 39 Washington Ave., P.O. Box 40, Pleasantville, N.Y. 10570. (800) 431-1934. VHS 1/2" cassette, 21 minutes. Most children get teased at some time, but this film examines what happens when the teasing gets out of hand, crosses the line, and becomes harassment. It also examines the dynamics behind teasing and being teased, and models effective responses to being harassed. Explores the issues of peer cruelty and teaches the importance of "finding allies" and "strength in numbers" in thwarting harassment through the power of mutual support. Suggested for grade levels 5-9.

Everybody's Different. Sunburst Communications, 39 Washington Ave., P.O. Box 40, Pleasantville, N.Y. 10570. (800) 431-1934. VHS 1/2" cassette, 14 minutes. With song lyrics that proclaim, "Everybody's different, no one's quite the same," this program celebrates individual differences. Helps the youngest students understand that everyone is different in some way, and that it's not only okay to be different, it can be very interesting. Includes excellent activities that are reproducible. Suggested for grade levels K-2.

How I Learned Not to Be Bullied. Sunburst Communications, 39 Washington Ave., P.O. Box 40, Pleasantville, N.Y. 10570. (800) 431-1934. Program helps students understand how their behavior and attitudes affect how others treat them. Explains why bullies act the way they do, provides strategies for dealing with a bully. Comes with teachers guide, student work sheets and send-home pages. Suggested for grades 2-4.

No More Teasing. Sunburst Communications, 39 Washington Ave., P.O. Box 40, Pleasantville, N.Y. 10570. (800) 431-1934. VHS 1/2" cassette, 14 minutes. Presents effective strategies kids can use to protect themselves against teasing or bullying. With the help of the "No More Teasing Team" — peer hosts who introduce common teasing situations and offer solutions — shows how students can change their own behavior to lessen teasing or bullying's impact. Includes excellent activities that are reproducible. Suggested for grade levels 2-4.

No One Quite like Me . . . Or You. Sunburst Communications, 39 Washington Ave., P.O. Box 40, Pleasantville, NY 10570. (800) 431-1934. VHS 1/2" cassette, 16 minutes. Encourages viewers to see differences as valuable, as something that makes each of us unique. But by also making it clear that all of us are alike in many ways, helps students learn to value differences in themselves and others. Suggested for grade levels 2-4.

Only One Me . . . Only One You. Sunburst Communications, 39 Washington Ave., P.O. Box 40, Pleasantville, N.Y. 10570. (800) 431-1934. VHS 1/2" 25 minutes. Helps students appreciate cultural or personal differences among peers — from the kid who hates sports to the one who speaks a foreign language to the one who is physically disabled. Shows students that in accepting the uniqueness of others, they learn to value themselves. Suggested for grade levels 2-4.

Prevent Violence with Groark: Groark Learns about Bullying. Plainview, N.Y.: The Bureau for At-Risk Youth. 1-800-99-YOUTH. Groark is playing with friends when two of them start teasing and picking on a third one. Groark joins in. When his friend goes off crying, Groark doesn't understand what happened until he learns from a group of real elementary school children how he and the others were being bullies, and how hurtful that was to the friend. Together they make peace with the friend they had picked on.

Respect Yourself and Others, Too. Sunburst Communications, 39 Washington Ave., P.O. Box 40, Pleasantville, N.Y. 10570. (800) 431-1934. VHS 1/2" cassette, 14 minutes. Teaches social sensitivity as a key step in promoting respect and understanding among students. Emphasizes the importance of respecting the rights and needs of others, illustrates the problems that result from put-downs, fighting, or ignoring others' feelings. Helps students develop empathy and discover that when they show respect for others, they increase their own self-respect. Includes excellent activities that are reproducible. Suggested for grade levels K-2.

Set Straight on Bullies. Malibu, Calif.: National School Safety Center (NSSC), 1988. (805) 373-9977. This video explores all sides of today's bullying problem. Shown through the eyes of a young bullying victim, it brings to light the damaging effect that bullying has on all who are involved — physical and psychological damage that can last a lifetime. Suggested for grades 4-6.

Sex, Power and the Workplace. Lifeguides, KCET Video, 4401 Sunset Blvd., Los Angeles, Calif., 90007. (800) 343-4727. VHS 1/2" cassette, 60 minutes. This is an excellent training film for educators and other employees about sexual harassment in the workplace. It provides the historical development of the definition of sexual harassment under Title VII. It includes the stories of the women who have filed suit and the outcomes. It also includes a section on the importance of staff awareness training in the prevention of sexual harassment.

Sexual Harassment: It's Hurting People. Sunburst Communications, 39 Washington Ave., P.O. Box 40, Pleasantville, N.Y. 10570. (800) 431-1934. VHS 1/2" cassette, 18 minutes. Four out of five students say they are sexually harassed often or occasionally. Defining such harassment as any unwelcome behavior of a sexual nature, the program makes it clear that harassment in or out of school is both demeaning and wrong. Shows harassers how their behavior hurts others, details the steps schools and students can take to bring sexual harassment to a halt. Suggested for grade levels 5-9.

Sexual Harassment: Minimize the Risk. McGrath Systems, 211 East Victoria St., Suite B, Santa Barbara, Calif. (805) 882-1212. VHS 1/2" cassette. This legally-based training video for educators and staff (K-college level) includes legal information on school district and personal liability; shows and tells how to investigate, including early detection, process and steps to handle complaints, and interview guidelines; and remedial/disciplinary actions.

Staff Development: Bullying at School Strategies for Prevention. Pleasantville, N.Y.: Sunburst Communications, 39 Washington Ave., P.O. Box 40, Pleasantville, N.Y. 10570. (800) 431-1934. Examines the pervasiveness of bullying in schools. Notes that bullying is often invisible and inaudible to school personnel, discusses how it differs from conflict or fights. Urges school staff to aim to foster a school climate where all children can develop confidence and trust. Offers effective strategies both for preventing bullying and for encouraging respect and responsibility among students. Suggested for teachers/administrators of grades K-6.

Stop Teasing Me. Sunburst Communications, 39 Washington Ave., P.O. Box 40, Pleasantville, N.Y. 10570. (800) 431-1934. VHS 1/2" cassette, 12 minutes. Helps young students understand how teasing affects other people's feelings. Using a lively music video, a spaceman narrator, and a robot who speaks in rhymes to reinforce the points made, this video makes it clear that "Teasing isn't fun — Not for anyone!" Emphasizes that no one likes a teaser or being teased, shows viewers that they can make amends for teasing by doing something nice for the person they teased. Suggested for grade levels K-2.

You Can Say No: Here's How. Sunburst Communications. 39 Washington Ave., P.O. Box 40, Pleasantville, N.Y. 10570. (800) 431-1934. VHS 1/2" cassette, 23 minutes. This film helps students realize they have the right to act in their own self interest. Using realistic situations, middle school students are taught the importance of acting assertively and standing up for their rights. Students are taught to determine what is best for them — what values to live by — and then proceed to defend them in a responsible, assertive manner. Suggested for grade levels 5-9.

Children's Books, Curricula, and Educational Resources

Bosch, Carl W. *Bully on the Bus.* Seattle: Parenting Press, Inc., 1988. "The Decision Is Yours" series book lets kids take an active part in deciding what happens on the bus on the way to school as well as the results of their choice, and gives them an opportunity to go back and choose a different ending. Suggested for children ages 7-11.

Cieloha, Dan, and Parker Page with Murray Suid. *Getting Along: A Program for Developing Skills in Cooperation, Caring for Others, Critical Thinking and Positive Conflict Resolution.* Circle Pines, Minn.: American Guidance Service, 1990. (800) 328-2560. This is a behavior management program as well as a social development curriculum, and includes teacher's materials and student activity sheets. The program gives children concrete alternatives to help them get their needs met in addition to helping them to control their aggressive impulses or destructive behavior. Suggested for grades K-4.

Crawford, Susan Hoy. *Beyond Dolls and Guns: 101 Ways to Help Children Avoid Gender Bias.* Portsmouth, N.H.: Heinemann, 1996. This book illuminates the many ways we unconsciously encourage gender bias, and offers concrete, easy-to-follow suggestions for raising boys and girls who can treat each other (and themselves) with dignity and respect, and can grow into adults who are equally caring, competent, and courageous.

Keller, Amy, and Gene Floersch. *The Value of Self-Respect.* Huntington, N.Y.: The Bureau For At-Risk Youth. 1-800-99-YOUTH. Helps children make smart choices by introducing easy-to-grasp and fun-to-use decision-making models. Once the steps to make good decisions are understood, children can face tough choices regarding drugs, peer pressure, honesty, school and personal values. Suggested for grades 4-8.

Keller, Amy, and Gene Floersch. *The Value of Respecting Others.* Huntington, N.Y.: The Bureau For At-Risk Youth. 1-800-99-YOUTH. Teaches children to accept themselves and others as having dignity and worth. The activities are designed to help students develop the tolerance and understanding needed to excel in today's culturally diverse society. An excellent resource to any multi-cultural curricula. Suggested for grades 4-8.

Kaufman, Gershen, and Lev Raphael. *Stick Up for Yourself!: Every Kid's Guide to Personal Power and Positive Self-Esteem.* Minneapolis, Minn.: Free Spirit Publishing, 1990. This book instructs children how to stick up for themselves with other kids, big sisters and brothers, and even with parents and teachers. Furthermore, it explains to kids how to do this without putting other people down and without getting into trouble. Suggested for kids ages 8-12 and also for teachers, counselors, and parents.

Levin, Diane. *Teaching Young Children in Violent Times: Building a Peaceable Classroom; A Preschool-Grade 3 Violence Prevention and Conflict Resolution Guide.* Dubuque, Iowa: Educators for Social Responsibility, 1994. This guide deepens understanding of the development roots of young people's thinking on issues ranging from conflict to prejudice to violence, explores the cultural content for violence in children's lives and offers practical activities and ideas to create a Peaceable Classroom.

Stein, Nan, and Lisa Sjostrom. *Bullyproof: A Teacher's Guide on Teasing and Bullying.* Wellesley, Mass.: Wellesley College Center for Research on

Women, 1996. A curriculum of activities on teasing and bullying prevention for fourth and fifth grade students.

Viorst, Judith. *Alexander and the Terrible, Horrible, No Good, Very Bad Day.* Atheneum, N.Y.: McClelland & Stewart, 1975. A children's book about a boy having a terrible day when nothing was going right. This book informs kids that there are other children that have bad days too.

Let's Talk About Bullies: A Violence Prevention Activities Book. Flushing, N.Y.: Promotional Slideguide, 1996. (718) 886-8408. Suggested for grades 3-5.

What To Do About Peer Pressure: An Educational Activity Book. Flushing, N.Y.: Promotional Slideguide, 1996. (718) 886-8408. Suggested for grades 3-5.

Be Yourself; Handling Peer Pressure: An Educational Activity Book. Flushing, N.Y.: Promotional Slideguide, 1996. (718) 886-8408. Suggested for grades 3-5.

Unit 2: Teasing, Bullying, and Sexual Harassment Prevention

Part B: Classroom Materials

Sexual Harassment Curriculum for Grades K-3

Goals

■ Students will learn that there are rules about how students and adults should behave toward each other in school so that this environment is a safe and positive place in which to learn.

■ Students will learn how to behave in ways that respect other people's feelings and will be helped to understand how their own behavior can make other people feel.

■ Students will learn what their rights are in school and how to protect those rights.

■ Students will learn the things about themselves that make them different, special, and worthy of good treatment. They will also learn to appreciate differences in others and treat them with respect as well.

Introducing the Topic

Explain to the students: It's your body. Nobody has a right to touch you or treat you in a way that makes you feel uncomfortable. This is important because you are all special and deserve good treatment.

We are going to practice how to tell and get help when someone makes you feel bad or hurts you in any way in school.

We are going to learn the rules in our school that help students behave in ways to make each other feel good, safe, and happy while learning in school.

Classroom Activities

1. **About Bullying and Teasing.** This activity defines bullying, teasing, and disrespectful behaviors that are not allowed in school. It also introduces School Behavior Rules, a sexual harassment policy presented in age-appropriate language for elementary school students.

2. **Suzie and the Playground.** This activity teaches the students empathy. One way to help students treat each other well is for them to think about how their behavior makes the other person feel. It is important to realize that the effects of harassment build up over time and escalate if not confronted.

3. **Assert Yourself.** This activity gives students an opportunity to practice being assertive so they can be prepared to use this skill to protect themselves.

4. **Bully Busters.** This activity teaches the importance of all students working together to help stop teasing and bullying in school, and

reinforces the value of friends and classmates helping each other. It also emphasizes the importance of telling an adult whenever bullying and teasing happens in order to prevent the behavior from reoccurring.

5. **Class Bill of Rights.** This activity provides the students in the class with an opportunity to make their classroom a safe and happy place to learn. They are asked to develop a list of rights that describes the way each person wants to be treated and the way each person in the class should treat others. Having a bill of rights can help students stand up for themselves, remind students what behaviors are not OK, and encourage others to stand up for their friends.

6. **People Packages.** This activity reinforces for students that they are special and unique. It encourages them to consider all the different parts that make up their special selves. It helps students to appreciate the differences in others.

Activity 1 – About Bullying and Teasing

Introduce School Behavior Rules

Explain to the students: Everyone learns best when they feel safe, happy, and good about themselves. We have special rules that will protect you called School Behavior Rules.

Lots of kids think that being teased and bullied are just part of going to school and you just have to put up with it. It is important for every student to know that no one here has to put up with disrespectful treatment. The adults are here to protect you and your rights.

Give the students a copy of the School Behavior Rules (Handout #1) and review. Explain that in order to follow these rules you need to be able to recognize bullying, teasing, and disrespectful behaviors that are not allowed in our school. This is the first step toward making your school a safe place. Once we understand it, we can do something about it.

Define Bullying

Bullying and teasing is a form of disrespectful behavior that can be physical such as hitting someone, verbal such as calling someone names, or emotional such as giving someone the silent treatment. The child or group of children who are doing the bullying or teasing end up having a lot of power to hurt others if the disrespectful behavior is not stopped. Sometimes it happens over and over again to one person and can cause that person to feel bad, hurt, and afraid to go to school. It can also happen to lots of different kids making it feel like school is not a place to go to where people can feel good about themselves.

Show the students a video that depicts various kinds of bullying and teasing behaviors to facilitate a discussion about specific behaviors that are not allowed.

Bullying Video

Bullies: Violence Cessation (see Unit 2A References: Sexual Harassment, Teasing, and Bullying Prevention Videos) is recommended for grades 1-3. An activity with related discussion questions follows. However, it would be helpful for the teacher to view the video before showing it to the students in order to be prepared with specific responses.

Before showing the video:

■ Ask the students to take special notice of the different examples of bullying behaviors mentioned in the video so that the class can develop a list afterwards.

■ Also ask that they pay attention to how it made the victims and witnesses of bullying feel.

After showing the video:

Discussion Questions:	Presenter's Responses:
Generate a list of bullying behaviors mentioned in the video. Ask the students to add any examples they have either experienced or witnessed since they have attended school here.	Encourage the following responses and inform the students that these behaviors are not allowed here: • making fun of someone • name calling • taking lunch money • knocking books out of hands • cornering someone • older kids beating up younger kids • ignoring another person • giving someone the silent treatment • tripping someone, hair pulling
How did the bullying make the kid(s) being bullied feel?	Bullying and teasing is not allowed in school because it can make someone feel unsafe and affect their ability to learn.
How did other students witnessing the bullying feel?	When other students saw what was happening it made them afraid too. This is why we have school behavior rules so that everyone is equally protected and can feel good when going to school.

Discussion Questions:	Presenter's Responses:
In the video, other students knew the bullies and the kids being bullied but didn't often tell adults about it. Why do you think they didn't tell?	Emphasize the importance of telling to get the behavior to stop. Often kids think it will only make things worse if they tell but the opposite is true. It gets worse if you don't.
Do you think if kids know who the bullies are and who is being bullied that students would tell and get help? Why or why not?	Explain that telling to get help is not tattling. By telling an adult you take the power to hurt someone else away from the bully.
If someone tells, who else are they protecting besides the student who is being bullied?	Telling protects the person being bullied, other students who may be the bully's next target, and even the person who is bullying because if the bully is stopped it can help him or her avoid getting into bigger trouble.
What can students do when they see bullying and teasing happening to someone else?	Reinforce that there is strength in numbers. It may be hard for one person to stand up to one or more kids especially if they are bigger, stronger, or threatening. But if a bunch of kids band together and speak up against mean behavior when they see it, it can really make a difference. Also a friend can help by offering to go with the person being teased for help. Any student who is a witness can go to an adult for help as well.

Handout #1
School Behavior Rules

Explain to the students that everyone learns best when they feel safe, happy, and good about themselves. We have special rules that protect you:

☺ No one is allowed to touch you in a way that makes you feel uncomfortable.

☺ No one is allowed to hurt you, or tease you and say things to you that make you feel bad about yourself or your body.

☺ No one is allowed to bully you. No one is allowed to say they will hurt you if you tell on them or don't do what they say.

☺ Everyone has the right to tell an adult and get help if they are teased, bullied, or hurt in any way.

Activity 2 – Suzie and the Playground

This activity encourages students to develop empathy as an important skill in promoting the respectful treatment of others. Often children do not consider the effect their behavior has on others when they are part of a group. One way to help students treat each other well is for each person to think about how their behavior makes the other person feel.

Explain

■ Although a little teasing by one person may not hurt someone much, lots of teasing by one person can make someone feel badly. In the same way, a little teasing by a group of people (children) can also hurt a lot.

■ If someone teases you, it is not your fault. The person who is doing the teasing is doing something wrong and is to blame.

■ Teasing and bullying hurt people's feelings and they are not allowed in our school.

■ If students feel uncomfortable, encourage them to respond to teasing by saying: "Stop that!" or "You are not allowed to do that in this school!"

■ Tell them that anytime they are teased or bullied they should tell a trusted adult in school and get help. Emphasize that telling to get help is not tattling.

Read the story to the students. Before reading the story ask the students to think about how Suzie's classmates made her feel in school.

> *Every day when Suzie goes out to play in the playground a group of boys makes fun of her. They call her names and chase her. The other girls laugh at the boys when this happens. Suzie doesn't play with anyone during recess anymore. She just goes off by herself and waits until it's over.*

> *Suzie used to love school but lately she hasn't been feeling the same way. Sometimes her stomach hurts before going to school, especially when she thinks about recess. Sometimes she can't do her work in school because she's worried about what will happen during recess.*

> *Sometimes Suzie thinks, "What's wrong with me? Maybe I did something wrong and that's why the other kids tease me."*

Discussion Questions for grades K-1:

■ How does Suzie feel when the other kids make fun of her?

■ How does the teasing change the way Suzie feels about school?

■ Why did her feelings change?

- Suzie thinks maybe something is wrong with her. Did Suzie do anything wrong here?
- What are the rules about teasing in our school?
- What should you do if someone teases you?
- What should you do if you see someone else being teased?

Discussion Questions for grades 2-3:

- How does Suzie feel when the other kids make fun of her?
- How does the teasing change the way Suzie feels about school? Why did her feelings change?
- How does the teasing affect the way she feels about herself?
- Why do you think the boys are teasing Suzie?
- Do you think the other kids realize how bad they are making Suzie feel?
- Suzie thinks maybe something is wrong with her. Did Suzie do something wrong?
- Does teasing like this ever happen here?
- Do the boys tease the girls here? Do the boys tease each other here? Give examples.
- Do the girls tease the boys? Do the girls tease each other here? Give examples.
- What are the rules about teasing in our school?
- What should you do if someone teases you?
- What should you do if you see someone else teased?

Activity 3 – Assert Yourself

Saying No Role-Play Activity

Explain that each person in the class will have a chance to practice being assertive. This means that they will learn how to show the other person that they really mean it when they say they do not want to be bullied or teased.

Prepare a set of index cards with written examples of touches and teasing or bullying comments that kids may experience in their daily lives in their interaction with their peers. As the teacher, be sure to include in your own observations examples of what the students do and say to each other. If the students are old enough, they may generate the examples from their own experiences. If the students have already participated in this activity when it was introduced in Unit 1B, Activity #3, refer back and add to the pile of cards already developed.

Encourage each child to take turns to show asserting themselves by:

- using their most important voice
- standing up straight and tall
- have a serious expression on your face
- look the person in the eyes
- saying what you want over and over again until they believe you

Instruct the children to pick a card and ask, "What would you say if someone tried to . . . "

- pull your hair in class?
- push you while walking in the hall?
- hit you on the playground?
- trip you on purpose?
- pinch you?
- make fun of you?

Encourage the students to practice asserting themselves and to keep practicing saying no whenever they need to with their classmates. Suggest that as the school year progresses, more cards can be added to the pile from things that happen in school and the class can play the game and practice again.

Activity 4 – Bully Busters

Explain

■ Kids need to learn how to "stand up" for themselves and others so that it really counts and makes a difference in how people treat each other.

■ Usually kids know who the bullies are and who is being teased or bullied more than adults do because they see it happening to other kids outside the classroom. If no one speaks up against the teasing or bullying the kids doing it get away with being mean to other kids. When this happens the bullies end up having a lot of power. They can keep making others feel bad just because they want to. This is bad power and it is used to hurt others.

■ Everyone here has the power to stop teasing and bullying when you see it. It's called peer power and it is a lot stronger than the bad power bullies use to hurt others. This is because the number of kids who see it happening are a much bigger group than the one or few kids who are actually doing the teasing or bullying. This larger group has a lot of power if they stick together to help others because there is strength in numbers.

Read the story to the class

Bert, Margo, and George are Bully Busters. Their school has a rule that says no one has the right to hurt others or make them feel bad because school is supposed to be a safe place. Bullying is definitely not allowed.

Bert, Margo, and George know what a bad thing it is to bully someone, and how it can hurt someone's feelings. They started the Bully Busters to make sure that everyone knew that bullying was against the rules. When they see someone being bullied, they go into action.

It was lunch time. Timmy's mom had put his favorite peanut butter cookies in his lunch bag and he had saved them for last. As he took out his cookies, Mike came over. Mike was bigger and older than Timmy, and much stronger.

"What 'ja got there, jerk?"

"Cookies," said Timmy.

"Good. I like cookies," said Mike, grabbing the bag and pushing Timmy aside.

Suddenly who should appear but the Bully Busters! Margo, Bert, and George surrounded Mike.

"Mike, you are being a bully. Bullying is bad and hurts other people," said George.

"Bullying is not allowed at our school," said Bert.

"We all have a right to feel safe here — and that includes our cookies!" said Margo.

When Bully Busters told their teacher Miss Maple about what happened at lunch, she thanked them. She said, "I am glad you remembered that telling to get help is not tattling. You did the right thing by telling. If you hadn't told about Mike, he could have tried to bully other kids. Now everyone is safer and Mike can be taught how not to bully anymore. Good job Bully Busters! It makes everyone in school feel safer when both kids and adults help to put a stop to bullying at school."

Discuss:

■ How do you think Timmy was feeling when Mike bullied him?

■ How do you think Timmy felt when the bully busters helped him out?

■ Why was it important for all Timmy's classmates that Mike's bullying be stopped?

■ Why was it important to tell Miss Maple about Mike?

■ How does telling help Mike out as well?

■ What could you and your friends do to help stop teasing or bullying if it happens to someone in your school ?

Assertiveness Role-Play Techniques

Explain: Just like the Bully Busters — Bert, Margo, and George — we are going to practice being bully busters by standing up together for other students when they need help, and by telling and adult.

If you participated in the Assert Yourself Activity (Unit 2B, Activity #3), the class may have already practiced asserting themselves. If this is the case, explain here is another chance to practice, this time as a group of students, asserting themselves together.

Each student in the group can take turns asserting themselves and "show they really mean it" by:

■ using your most important voice

■ standing up straight and tall

■ having a serious expression on your face

■ look the person in the eyes

■ saying what you want over and over again until they believe you

Ask for volunteers to play the following roles:

■ one student role plays the bully Mike

■ one student role plays Timmy

- one student role plays the teacher, Miss Maple

The rest of the class takes turns coming up in front of the class in groups of three or more students to role play the Bully Busters, Bert, Margo, and George. Instruct each group to act out:

- the Bully Busters "showing they really mean it" when Mike bullies Timmy
- the Bully Busters "showing they really mean it" by telling Miss Maple

Reinforce during the role plays that a group of kids trying to help out has a lot more power than the bully when they stick together, speak out, and when they tell an adult they need help.

Activity 5 – Class Bill of Rights

One way to encourage students to act respectfully to each other is to help them think in terms of having a right to be treated in ways that make them feel good, safe, and happy in school.

Reinforce

- We have learned we all have a right to good treatment in school.
- We also learned no one can take these rights from you. You are protected by the rules in your school that tell people how to behave toward each other.
- Understanding your rights can help you stand up for yourself and help others.

Activity

Explain: We are now going to have our own class rules called our Class Bill of Rights. These rules will protect your rights and will help us to remember the right ways to treat each other in our classroom. It will help you learn how to speak up if someone does not treat you right.

It is important to listen to your feelings. They tell you if something is OK or not OK for you. If you feel badly because of the way someone treats you in school or class, listen to your feelings. It is not OK for another person to make you feel badly or hurt you in any way. It's against the rules in our Class Bill of Rights.

If someone is treating you badly you can tell them, "Stop it! You broke the class rules. No one is allowed to hurt anyone in this class." If you see someone being hurt or not being nice to another person in class — even if it's not you — you can tell them they are not acting right. We all need to work together to make this a safe and happy place to learn.

The Class Bill of Rights can be used to remind students when rules are broken and can serve as positive reinforcement when students show respect and good treatment toward each other in class. It also provides a way to teach students how to assert themselves. Review with the class and refer to as often as needed throughout the school year.

Prepare a poster of the Class Bill of Rights to display in the classroom. A sample poster follows on the next page.

Class Bill of Rights

Everyone in this class deserves good treatment. We are all special and different from each other. We pledge to respect each others' rights.

I Have a Right to	This Means No One Has a Right to
I have a right to be happy and to be treated well in this room.	This means no one has a right to tease me, laugh at me, make fun of me, or hurt my feelings.
I have a right to be myself and to be different and unique in this room.	This means no one has a right to treat me unfairly or differently because I am black or white, fat or thin, tall or short, boy or girl, or different from another person in any way.
I have a right to be safe in this room and not be hurt by other students or by adults who work in my school.	This means no one has a right to bully me, hit me, kick me, push me, pinch me, hurt my body, or touch me in any way I don't like.
I have a right to my own feelings, thoughts and ideas, and to stand up for myself when I feel I need to say no or disagree.	This means no one has a right to tell me it's my fault or I am wrong if I feel bad or hurt, or if I choose not to listen to other people who tell me to do bad things.
I have a right to get help from my teacher or any trusted adult if someone hurts me, hurts my feelings, scares me, touches me in ways I don't like, or makes me feel badly.	This means no one has a right to make me promise not to tell when someone hurts me or makes me keep a bad secret.
I have a right to privacy, my own body, and my own things in this room.	This means no one has a right to touch the things that belong to me including my body and the things in my desk if I don't want them to.

**Remember if someone treats you in a way that
is not right and makes you feel hurt, say:**

"Stop It!"

"Don't Do That to Me!"

"You Are Not Allowed to Hurt Me. It's Against the Rules."

and

Tell And Get Help.

Activity 6 – People Packages

This activity is designed to be repeated throughout the school year and provides positive reinforcement that students are special, unique, and worthy of good treatment. It encourages them to consider all the different parts of who they are that make up their special selves. It helps students appreciate what makes them different from others and the differences in others.

Reinforce

- Remember when we looked into the Magic Box (Unit 1B, Activity 1). We saw something special. It was you. We then talked about how there is no one else like you in the whole wide world and that it's important to take care of and protect our special selves.

- We are going to make our own boxes called People Packages. Instead of a mirror, we will put in our boxes things inside of us that makes each of us special, unique, and different. Your picture will be on the outside of the box.

- This box is important because it can help us learn things about ourselves that make us special and help us feel good about ourselves. It can help us remember that we all have a right to good treatment.

Activity

Ask the students to bring in a box they have decorated at home with a picture of themselves pasted on the cover. It should be bigger than a shoe box so that it can be used throughout the school year.

At this point have the students put something inside their box that is unique about their appearance such as their thumb print, a tape of their voice, a sample of their handwriting, or a lock of hair. Explain that the object they placed in the box is unique and a part of them. There is no other one like it in the whole world. It is different and special just like each of us.

After placing the object in the box, close it and say, "When you look at the box, can you tell what's inside? When you look at a person, can you tell what's inside of them? No. You can only tell what a person is really like by getting to know them and getting to know all the things about them that make them special, different, and unique."

Tell the students they are going to be able to put many different things in their boxes all year long. Sometimes it may be their art work, what they write, something about their family, the holidays they celebrate, their ideas, feelings, likes and dislikes. Each time they do, it can be a reminder that all the different things inside of us make all of us special, and worthy of good treatment.

Whenever the students work with their boxes, it can be a good time to review the Class Bill of Rights or the School Behavior Rules. Encourage them to review the rules so that they never forget to protect their rights and the rights of others.

Sexual Harassment Curriculum for Grades 4-6

Goals

- Students will learn there are rules about how students and adults should behave toward each other in school so that this environment is a safe and positive place in which to learn.

- Students will learn how to behave in ways that respect other people's feelings and will be helped to understand how their own behavior can make other people feel.

- Students will learn what their rights are in school and how to protect those rights.

- Students will learn the things about themselves that make them different, special, and worthy of good treatment. They will also learn to appreciate differences in others and treat them with respect as well.

Introducing the Topic

Explain: It's your body. Nobody has a right to touch you or treat you in a way that makes you feel uncomfortable. This is important because you are all special and deserve good treatment.

We are going to practice how to tell and get help when someone makes you feel bad or hurts you in any way in school.

We are going to learn the rules in our school that help students behave in ways to make each other feel good, safe, and happy while learning in school.

Classroom Activities

7. **About Bullying and Teasing.** This activity defines bullying, teasing, and disrespectful behaviors that are not allowed in school. It also introduces School Behavior Rules which is a sexual harassment policy presented in age-appropriate language for elementary school students.

8. **Unhappy at Lunch.** This activity teaches the students empathy by encouraging students to think about how their behavior makes the other person feel. It also provides an opportunity for the students to role play and practice being assertive when confronting teasing.

9. **Peer Power.** This activity teaches students the importance of onlookers standing up for others so that it really counts and makes a difference in how people treat each other here. Students discuss what-if situations and survey what is happening in their school. It emphasizes the importance of telling an adult whenever bullying and teasing happens in order to prevent the behavior from reoccurring.

10. **Assert Yourself.** This activity gives students an opportunity to practice being assertive so they can be prepared to use this skill to protect themselves. It introduces two handouts, Assertiveness Techniques and Assertiveness Techniques Checklist.

11. **Sexual Harassment Is Against the Law.** This activity addresses sexual or gender-based teasing and bullying. It explains the law, defines sexual harassment, and includes a video discussion and story about a student who is being sexually harassed.

12. **Class Bill of Rights.** This activity provides the students in the class with an opportunity to make their classroom a safe and happy place to learn. They are asked to develop a list of rights that describes the way each person wants to be treated and the way each person in the class should treat others. Having a bill of rights can help students stand up for themselves, remind students what behaviors are not OK, and encourage others to stand up for their friends.

13. **People Packages.** This activity reinforces for students they are special and unique. It encourages them to consider all the different parts that make up their special selves. It helps students to appreciate the ways they are different from others and to appreciate the differences in others.

Activity 7 — About Bullying and Teasing

Introduce School Behavior Rules

- Explain: Everyone learns best when they feel safe, happy, and good about themselves. We have special rules that protect you called School Behavior Rules.

- Lots of kids think being teased and bullied are just part of going to school and you just have to put up with it. It is important for every student to know that no one here has to put up with disrespectful treatment. The adults are here to protect you and your rights.

- Give the students a copy of the School Behavior Rules (Handout #1) and review. Explain that in order to follow these rules you need to be able to recognize bullying, teasing, and disrespectful behaviors that are not allowed in our school. This is the first step towards making your school a safe place. Once we understand what it is, we can do something about it.

Define Bullying

Bullying and teasing is a form of disrespectful behavior that can be physical such as hitting someone, verbal such as calling someone names, or emotional such as giving someone the silent treatment. The child or group of children who are doing the bullying or teasing end up having a lot of power to hurt others if the disrespectful behavior is not stopped. Sometimes it happens over and over again to one person and can cause that person to feel bad, hurt, and afraid to go to school. Sometimes it can also happen to lots of different kids making it feel like school is not a place where people can feel good about themselves.

Show the students a video that depicts various kinds of bullying and teasing behaviors to facilitate a discussion about specific behaviors that are not allowed.

Video: *Set Straight on Bullies*

The video entitled *Set Straight on Bullies* (see Unit 2A Resources: Sexual Harassment, Teasing, and Bullying Prevention Videos) is recommended for grades 4-6 and related discussion questions follow. It would be helpful for the teacher to view the video before showing it to the students in order to be prepared with responses specific to the video.

Before showing the video, ask the students:

■ to take special notice of the different examples of bullying behaviors mentioned in the video so that the class can develop a list of them afterwards,

■ to pay attention to how it made the victims and witnesses of bullying feel.

After showing the video, discuss:

Discussion Questions:	Presenter's Responses:
Generate a list of bullying behaviors mentioned in the video. Ask the students to add to the list any additional examples they have either experienced or witnessed since they have attended school here.	Encourage the following responses and inform the students that these behaviors are not allowed here. • making fun of someone • name calling • taking lunch money • knocking books out of hands • cornering someone • older kids beating up younger kids • ignoring another person • giving someone the silent treatment • tripping someone, hair pulling
How did the bullying make the kid(s) being bullied feel? How did it make other students witnessing the bullying feel?	Bullying and teasing is not allowed in school because it can make someone feel unsafe and affect their ability to learn. When other students saw what was happening it made them afraid too. This is why we have school behavior rules so that everyone is equally protected and can feel good when going to school.

In the video, other students knew who the bullies were and the kids were being bullied but didn't often tell adults about it. Why do you think they didn't tell?

Emphasize the importance of telling to stop the behavior. Often kids think it will only make things worse if they tell but the opposite is true. It gets worse if you don't.

Do you think if kids know who the bullies are and who is being bullied, that students would tell and get help? Why or why not? If someone tells, who else are they protecting besides the student who is being bullied?

Explain that telling to get help is not tattling. By telling an adult you take the power to hurt someone else away from the bully. Telling protects the person being bullied, all other students who may be the bully's next target, and even the person who is bullying — because if the bully is stopped it can help him or her avoid getting into bigger trouble.

What can students do when they see bullying and teasing happening to someone else?

Reinforce that there is strength in numbers. It may be hard for one person to stand up to one or more kids especially if they are bigger, stronger, or threatening. But if a bunch of kids band together and speak up against mean behavior when they see it, it can really make a difference. Also a friend can help by offering to go with the person being teased for help. Any student who is a witness can go to an adult for help as well.

Handout #1
School Behavior Rules

Explain to the students that everyone learns best when they feel safe, happy, and good about themselves. We have special rules that will protect you:

☺ No one is allowed to touch you in a way that makes you feel uncomfortable.

☺ No one is allowed to hurt you, tease you, or say things to you that make you feel badly about yourself or your body.

☺ No one is allowed to bully you. No one is allowed to say they will hurt you if you tell on them or don't do what they say.

☺ Everyone has the right to tell an adult and get help if they are teased, bullied, or hurt in any way.

Activity 8 — Unhappy at Lunch

Explain

This activity encourages students to develop empathy as an important skill that promotes the respectful treatment of others. Often children do not consider the effect their behavior has on others when they are part of a group. One way to help students treat each other well is for each person to think about how their behavior makes the other person feel.

Read the story to the students: Ask them to think about how Jenny's classmates made her feel in school.

One day at lunch, Sara, one of "the popular girls," started teasing Jenny. When Jenny tried to ignore her, Sara told the other girls a secret about Jenny that was not true. When she said, "I did not!" they all started laughing and making fun of her. Since then, this group of girls has teased Jenny everyday at lunch, pointing at her and calling her names. The other girls laugh when this happens, even the girls Jenny thought were her friends. Jenny tries to finish lunch as quickly as possible, and then goes off by herself until it's time for class.

She used to love school, but lately she hasn't been feeling the same way. Sometimes her stomach hurts before going to school when she thinks about lunch period. Sometimes she can't do her work in the morning classes because she is worried about what might happen at lunch. Sometimes Jenny thinks, "What's wrong with me? Maybe I did something wrong and that's why the other girls tease me."

Discuss:	Presenter's Responses:
How does Jenny feel when the other girls make fun of her?	Jenny feels bad and her feelings are hurt when she is teased.
How does the teasing change the way Jenny feels about school? Why did her feelings change?	She feels worried and scared that it will happen again. She has trouble doing her school work and is worried about that too.
How does the teasing affect the way she feels about herself?	She thinks that maybe there is something wrong with her and that is why others tease her. The reason why teasing is against the rules at school is because it makes people feel badly, it is unsafe, and it hurts.

113

Discuss:	Presenter's Responses:
Why do you think the "popular girls" are teasing Jenny? Does this ever happen here?	Boys and girls tease because everyone else is doing it and it makes them feel like they are part of the group. They may only intend to joke or kid around and may not realize how much they are hurting the other person by teasing.
Do you think each girl in the group realizes how bad they are making Jenny feel?	Although a little teasing by one person may not hurt someone very much, lots of teasing by one person can make someone feel very bad. In the same way, a little teasing by a group of people (children) can also hurt a lot.
Why did the other girls laugh at the teasing?	The girls laughed because they thought they would not be the next targets if they acted like it didn't bother them. Actually it gives the opposite message and can only makes things worse. It can give permission to treat the other girls the same way too. It makes the "popular girls" think they're doing nothing wrong and that the teasing is OK.
Jenny thinks maybe something is wrong with her because she is teased. Did Jenny do anything wrong ?	No! Jenny did nothing wrong. It's not her fault. The girls who teased her are to blame. They broke the rule in school about not teasing and hurting other people.
The first time Jenny was teased, what could she have done? What should you do if you are teased in school?	It is important to tell and get help even if the teasing or bullying happens only once. If ignored these behaviors will get worse.

Activity 9 — Peer Power

Introduce this activity by asking the class who agrees or disagrees with the following statements:

- **Everyone** has a right not to be bullied or teased in our school.
- **No one** has a right to bully or tease another person in our school.

The likelihood is that the students will unanimously agree with both statements. Tell the students that even though everyone believes this, we know that bullying and teasing still happens in our school. This is because kids need to learn how to "stand up" for themselves and others so that it really counts and makes a difference in how people treat each other here.

Explain

Usually kids know who the bullies are and who is being teased or bullied more than adults do because they see it happening to other kids outside the classroom. If no one speaks up against the teasing or bullying the kids doing it get away with being mean to other kids. When this happens, the bullies end up having a lot of power. They can keep making others feel bad just because they want to. This is bad power and it is used to hurt others.

Everyone here has the power to stop teasing and bullying when you see it. It's called peer power and it is a lot stronger than the bad power bullies use to hurt others. This is because the number of kids who see it happening are a much bigger group than the one or few kids who are actually doing the teasing or bullying. This larger group has a lot of power if they stick together to help others because there is strength in numbers.

Reinforce

Bullies have the power and control over other students when:

- ☐ other kids laugh or join in when they see it happening
- ☐ other kids stay silent when they see it happening
- ☐ other kids don't tell an adult and get help

Each person can get the power and control back from the bully by:

- ☐ not laughing or joining in when you see it happening
- ☐ speaking up against the bullying when you see it
- ☐ getting others to join you to speak up against the bullying when you see it
- ☐ telling an adult about the bullying you witnessed or experienced
- ☐ going with a friend to tell an adult about the bullying your friend experienced

Present what-if situations. Refer to the list above about what you can do to get the power back from the bully and discuss how you can use peer power to help make things better in each situation.

Situation #1

At the bus stop Billy was picked on frequently by another kid who was older and bigger. The bigger kid called him names, threatened to take his lunch money, and threw his books in the mud. The other kids just watched and didn't say anything. Billy just tried to avoid him and finally the bigger kid just stopped bothering him. Billy never reported him and the other day he saw the bigger kid picking on someone else during recess at school. He remembers how bad he felt when it was happening to him but he was afraid to say something because he was worried the bully would start up with him again.

Situation #2

Every day at recess a group of older and bigger kids hog the football and playing field. If they get to recess after other kids are already playing on the field, they just tell them to get lost and take the ball. The other kids are told they just have to listen or else. Jeremy loves to play football but he is afraid to be the only one to stand up to these kids.

Situation #3

Amy is bossy but what makes it worse it that she's popular too and the other girls go along with whatever she says. One day Amy talked her other friends into giving Pam "the silent treatment." When Karen spoke up and said it wasn't right, Amy said she better go along with it or she'll be next.

Student Survey

- Explain now that everyone understands about peer power we are going to break up into groups and discuss what's happening here at our school.
- Each group will be given a list of discussion questions about bullying and teasing. Discussion questions in How Kids See It (Handout #2) is on the following page.
- Ask some students in each group to take notes about what the group says. When the class comes back together have each group share their comments with the class as a whole.
- Instruct the students not to get personal and not to mention any student's name during the discussion.
- Students will have a chance to tell privately and get help later. Explain that the handout Teasing and Bullying Student Response Form will be provided for this purpose at the end of the activity.

■ For now it is just important to talk about how kids see it. It will help us try and figure out together if there are situations that exist in our school where using peer power can make a difference.

Handout #2
How Kids See It

Discuss

In this school, are there any kids that push other kids around and act like they have more rights than other students? Describe what happens but don't use the name of any students when you do.

If the answer is yes, where does it happen in our school? (bus? in the lunchroom? recess? girl or boy's bathroom? locker room?) How often does it happen? Does it happen to one particular kid, a few kids, or lots of kids?

Are there any adults around when it happens? If yes, what do the adults do about it?

What do the students who are being bullied do about it?

What do the students who are watching it do about it?

In the examples you discussed in your group, how can peer power help?

Handout #3
Bullying and Teasing Student Response Form

Please check one of the statements below about needing help with teasing or bullying:

☐ I do not need help with teasing or bullying right now.

☐ I am being teased or bullied and need help.

☐ I am worried about a friend who is being teased or bullied.

☐ I used to be teased or bullied and it has stopped. Now the person is doing it to someone else.

☐ I have seen other kids being teased or bullied and I don't want it to happen to anyone else.

Who would you like to talk to and get help:

☐ my teacher

☐ school principal

☐ school nurse

☐ another adult in school I trust _____

Student's Name _____

Activity 10 – Assert Yourself

Assertiveness Techniques

Introduce the activity to the class by explaining that everyone needs to practice asserting themselves with adults and their peers in everyday life experiences so they can be prepared to use this skill to protect themselves. Review with the class the Assertiveness Techniques (Handout #4) and explain that these are things you can do to help assert yourself in order to be taken seriously.

Break the class into small groups. Refer to the list of examples that were developed during Activity 9, Peer Power. In this activity the students participated in a student survey about what is happening in their own school while using the How Kids See It handout. Give each group two situations to work with from this survey. For each situation, using the Assertiveness Techniques as a guide, have the students discuss what to say and what to do when

- one or more students do not want to join their friends in the teasing and speak out against it, and

- a student stands up for him or herself when teased.

Using the suggestions generated from the groups ask several pairs of students to role play responding assertively in front of the class.

Distribute the Assertiveness Technique Checklist (Handout #5) and instruct the class to use it when observing the role plays. Then discuss which techniques were most helpful, work best in specific situations, and need the most practice.

Handout #4
Assertiveness Techniques[*]

Assertive Body Language

- Body posture: Stand straight and tall.

- Facial expression: Look serious and do not smile.

- Eye contact: Look directly at the person to whom you are speaking.

Verbal Assertive Skills

- Say no: Actually say the word "no" rather than using weaker phrases such as "I don't think so."

- Use your important voice: The way you say no or the way you refuse makes a difference in whether you are taken seriously. Use a strong voice to be believed.

- Don't give excuses: Tell the person exactly how you feel.

- Say no over and over again: Keep saying no until the person listens to you and believes you really mean it.

- Use "I" statements: Say "I want" you to stop what your doing.

*From Marjorie Fink, *Adolescent Sexual Assault and Harassment Prevention Curriculum* (Holmes Beach, Fla.: Learning Publications, 1995), 194-95.

Handout #5
Assertiveness Technique Checklist

	Yes	No
Body Language		
Stand straight and tall	☐	☐
Look serious	☐	☐
Eye contact	☐	☐
Verbal Skills		
Clearly say no	☐	☐
Use important voice	☐	☐
Say no again and again	☐	☐
"I" statements	☐	☐
No excuses	☐	☐

Activity 11 – Sexual Harassment Is Against the Law

It is recommended that the prevention program include material about sexual or gender-based teasing and bullying when fifth and/or sixth grade students present these behaviors in school and especially when they interface with older students because they attend middle rather than elementary school.

Explain

As part of the civil rights act there is a federal law stating no one is allowed to discriminate against you or treat you differently based on your race, your religion, your ethnic background, or your gender.

Gender or sex discrimination means that it is illegal for you to be treated differently in school just because you are a male or female student. For example your school can not teach only math to the boys and only English to girls. Both girls and boys have a right to play sports in your school.

Under this law, teasing and bullying that is sexual in nature is illegal too if it interferes with a student's ability to learn and participate in activities. It is against the law for a student to harasses another student, for an adult who works in school to harass a student, or for a student to harass an adult. This is called sexual harassment and it is also against our school behavior rules like other kinds of teasing and bullying.

Review the School Behavior Rules (Handout #1). Explain that in order to follow these rules and help protect you against sexual harassment you need to be able to recognize disrespectful behaviors that are sexual or gender based and not allowed in our school.

Show the students a video depicting various behaviors that constitute sexual harassment to facilitate a discussion about specific behaviors that are not allowed.

Video — *Sexual Harassment: It's Hurting People*

This video (see Unit 2A References: Sexual Harassment, Teasing, and Bullying Prevention Videos), appropriate for grades 5-8, shows examples of unwanted sexual attention, comments, and physical touching that happens to both the boys and girls in school.

Ask students to take special notice of the different sexual harassment examples mentioned in the video so that the class can develop a list on the board after viewing the video. When generating the list include specific examples that can happen to girls and specific examples that can happen to boys.

Ask if any of these or other kinds of harassing behaviors are a problem for the girls in this school? for the boys in this school? If you identify additional behaviors add them to the list.

Explain that these behaviors are not allowed and are against the school behavior rules. It is not OK for a student or adult to behave in these ways toward any child in school. These behaviors are not allowed in the classroom, the halls, the bathroom, the lunchroom, the lockers, on school grounds, on the school bus, or school-sponsored trips or events. Emphasize that if anyone is experiencing any of these kinds of disrespectful behaviors it is very important to go to a trusted adult in school for help. They will help you and make sure that your right to go to school in a safe place is protected. Anyone behaving this way in school will be disciplined because your school takes sexual harassment and your safety seriously.

Read Stacey's Story to the Group. This activity reinforces everyone's right to fully participate in school activities and emphasizes the important role of bystanders in its prevention.

Stacey recently joined the band and has band practice two days a week. The only way for her to get to the music room is to pass a group of boys who hang out at their lockers after lunch. The first couple of times Stacey went to practice, the boys whistled and made kissing noises at her. Since then, she has tried to always walk to practice with a group of girls, but it hasn't helped. The boys continue to single out Stacey, yelling "It's Stacey's time" when they see her coming and then making comments about how her body looks. Their comments are getting worse and more personal each time she walks by. The other girls stepped up their pace and rush past the boys as fast as they can. Stacey hasn't told anyone, but she is thinking of dropping out of the band.

Discuss
- Why did Stacey ignore the boys?
- Why did the other girls laugh?
- How did the boys make Stacey feel?
- If you were Stacey's friend how could you help her?
- Should Stacey drop out of the band?
- Should Stacey report what has happened to her?
- Would this be considered a case of serious harassment here? Why?
- How could the staff at Stacey's school help her?

Reinforce
- It's important to let someone know when their behavior bothers you in order that the behavior doesn't get worse.
- Each of us has a responsibility to think about how even one comment can be extremely hurtful because it can be one of many that add up.
- Harassment is serious when it continues over a period of time and makes you feel badly about school. It is also serious if an adult in school harasses a student. Stacey has a right to go to class and feel sale in school. It is

against the law if Stacey can't participate in a school activity or class because of harassment.

- If harassment happens, any one of you could be the one to try to speak up against it or try to stop it by reporting to a trusted adult in school. Distribute the Sexual Harassment Student Response Form (Handout #6) and explain that students will be able check off whether or not someone needs help. The form is available any time someone needs it during the school year.

- The chosen adult will help you by making sure the behavior stops and doesn't happen again to you or other students.

Handout #6
Sexual Harassment Student Response Form

Please check one of the statements below about needing help with touching, comments, teasing, or bullying of a sexual nature:

☐ I do not need help right now.

☐ I am being sexually harassed and need help.

☐ I am worried about a friend who is being sexually harassed.

☐ I used to be harassed and it has stopped. Now the person is doing it to someone else.

☐ I have seen other kids being harassed and I don't want it to happen to anyone else.

Who would you like to talk to and get help:

☐ my teacher

☐ school principal

☐ school nurse

☐ another adult in school I trust _____

Student's Name _____

Activity 12 — Class Bill of Rights

One way to encourage students to treat each other with respect is to help them think in terms of having a right to be treated in ways that make them feel good, safe, and happy in school.

Reinforce

- We have learned that we all have a right to good treatment in school.
- We also learned that no one can take these rights from you. They are protected by the rules in your school that tell people how to behave toward each other.
- Understanding your rights can help you stand up for yourself and help others.

Activity

Explain: We are now going to have our own class rules called our Class Bill of Rights. These rules will protect your rights and will help us to remember the right ways to treat each other in our classroom. It will help you learn how to speak up if someone does not treat you "right."

It is important to listen to your feelings. They tell you if something is OK or not OK for you. If you feel bad because of the way someone treats you in school or class, listen to your feelings. It is not OK for another person to make you feel bad or hurt you in any way. It's against the rules in our Class Bill of Rights.

If someone is treating you badly you can tell them, "Stop it! You broke the class rules. No one is allowed to hurt anyone in this class." If you see someone being hurt or not being nice to another person in class — even if it's not you — you can tell them that they are not acting right. We all need to work together to make this a safe and happy place to learn.

The Class Bill of Rights can be used to remind students when rules are broken and can serve as positive reinforcement when students show respect and good treatment toward each other in class. It also provides a way to teach students how to assert themselves. Review with the class and refer to as often as needed throughout the school year.

Develop with the students their own class bill of rights. Either address the class as a whole or break the class into small groups and discuss which rights are important to them and should be included. Incorporate the rights chosen by the students along with those listed in the sample poster on the next page.

Prepare a poster of the Class Bill of Rights and display it in the classroom.

Class Bill of Rights

Everyone in this class deserves good treatment. We are all different from each other and special people. We pledge to respect each others' rights.

I Have a Right to	This Means No One Has a Right to
I have a right to be happy and to be treated well in this room.	This means that no one has a right to tease me, laugh at me, make fun of me, or hurt my feelings.
I have a right to be myself and to be different and unique in this room.	This means that no one has a right to treat me unfairly or differently because I am black or white, fat or thin, tall or short, boy or girl or different from another person in any way.
I have a right to be safe in this room and not be hurt by other students or by adults who work in my school.	This means that no one has a right to bully me, hit me, kick me, push me, pinch me, hurt my body, or touch me in any way I don't like.
I have a right to my own feelings, thoughts, and ideas and to stand up for myself when I feel I need to say no or disagree.	This means no one has a right to tell me it's my fault or I am wrong if I feel bad or hurt, or if I choose not to listen to other people who tell me to do bad things.
I have a right to get help from my teacher or any trusted adult if some-one hurts me, hurts my feelings, scares me, touches me in ways I don't like, and makes me feel bad.	This means no one has a right to make me promise not to tell when someone hurts me or makes me keep a bad secret.
I have a right to privacy, my own body, and my own things in this room.	This means no one has a right to touch the things that belong to me including my body and the things in my desk if I don't want them to.

**Remember if someone treats you in a way that
is not right and makes you feel hurt, say:**

"Stop It!"

"Don't Do That to Me!"

"You Are Not Allowed to Hurt Me. It's Against the Rules."

and

Tell and Get Help.

Activity 13 – People Packages

This activity is designed to be positive reinforcement throughout the school year. It reinforces for students that they are special, unique and worthy of good treatment. It encourages them to consider all the different parts of who they are that make up their special selves. It helps students appreciate what makes them different from others and the differences in others.

Explain

■ Remember when we looked into the Magic Box (Unit 1B, Activity #1). We saw something special. It was you. We then talked about how there is no one else like you in the whole wide world and that it's important to take care of and protect our special selves.

■ We are going to make our own boxes called People Packages. Instead of a mirror, we will put in our boxes all the things that are inside of us that makes each of us special, unique and different. Your picture will be on the outside of the box.

■ This box is important because it can help us learn things about ourselves that make us special and help us feel good about ourselves. It can help us remember that we all have a right to good treatment.

Activity

Ask the students to bring in a box that they have decorated at home with a picture of themselves pasted on the cover. It should be bigger than a shoe box so that it can be used throughout the school year.

It this point have the students put something inside their package that is unique about their appearance such as their thumb print, a tape of their voice, a sample of their handwriting, a lock of hair. Explain that the object that they placed in the box is unique and a part of them. There is no other one like it in the whole world. It is different and special just like each of us.

After placing the object in the box and closing it ask: "When you look at the box, can you tell what's inside? When you look at a person, can you tell what's inside of them? No. You can only tell what a person is really like by getting to know them and getting to know all the things about them that make them special, different and unique."

Tell the students they are going to be able to put many different things in their packages all year long. Sometimes it may be their art work, what they write, something about their family, the holidays they celebrate, their ideas, feelings, likes and dislikes. Each time they do, it can be a reminder that all the different things inside of us make all of us special, and worthy of good treatment.

Whenever the students work with their packages, it can be a good time to review the Class Bill of Rights or the Student Behavior Policy. Encourage them to review the rules so that they never forget to protect their rights and the rights of others.

Unit 3: Child Abduction Prevention

Part A: Resource Materials for Educators

Note to Presenters

The third and final unit is dedicated to non-family abduction prevention. According to the May 1990 *National Incidence Studies of Missing, Abducted, Runaway, Throwaway Children in America,* stranger abduction is surprisingly low. There are about 50 million children in America. Approximately 4,600 children are taken by strangers annually, with 200-300 long-term kidnapping involving serious harm to the child. Of these, approximately all but 150 children are returned. It is estimated that each year 100 children are murdered after being abducted by a stranger. The likelihood is small that an individual child will be abducted and even less that a child will be murdered.

A U.S. Department of Justice study in 1997 analyzed child abductions resulting in murder, emphasizing the vulnerability of all children and the importance of teaching self-protection skills. This study focused on the kidnapping and murder of children under age 18 from the late 1970s to mid-1994. Disproving old law-enforcement assumptions that many child abductions were due to extortion and ransom, the study found that 58 percent of the victims were within a quarter-mile of home when their killer accosted them and that in two-thirds of the prosecuted cases, the abductor either lived nearby, was engaged in some athletic or social activity in the neighborhood, or worked or conducted business in the neighborhood. The report said that 53 percent of the 419 people convicted or charged in these killings were strangers to the slain children and that 39 percent were friends or acquaintances. Specific children were not targeted for victimization, the abductors "were more like killers-in-waiting given the right opportunity coupled with an available child, they were more likely to spring into action." Of the victims studied, 70 percent were females and the average age was 11.

Many states are requiring that abduction prevention education — like child sexual abuse prevention education — be taught in the schools on the elementary school level. In the case of child sexual abuse, this often is mandated because of the high incidence of child sexual abuse and because prevention education is known to reduce a child's vulnerability to being or continuing to be sexually abused. In the case of child abduction, preparing a child to protect themselves from abduction can greatly reduce a child's vulnerability because abduction by a stranger or an acquaintance is a crime of opportunity. Although the numbers are relatively low of actual abductions, there are about 115,000 reported attempted abductions yearly. For some reason these children were able to get away and protect themselves. Once again, as educators you are in the unique position to ensure that all children acquire these necessary skills.

While each unit is written to stand alone as an individual prevention program, when taught as part of a comprehensive safety prevention program, it is recommended that abduction prevention be taught as the last unit. When taught sequentially — child sexual abuse prevention first, sexual harassment

Part A: Resource Materials for Educators

135

prevention second and abduction prevention third — students benefit greatly from the reinforcement of skills that each program builds upon.

It especially is important to teach child sexual abuse prevention before introducing abduction prevention because the perpetrator is most often someone the child knows and does not involve abduction by a stranger or a casual acquaintance. Children are more likely to understand they have a right to say no to uncomfortable touches even to someone they know well and love when the issue is not confused by learning about stranger danger at the same time. Once they learn these skills the concepts should be applied to abduction prevention so that children can recognize that touching by a stranger or acquaintance is definitely a bad touch and dangerous. The concepts they have already learned in Unit 1 can then be reinforced — that their body is their own, no one has a right to touch them in ways that make them feel uncomfortable, they have a right to say no to adults to protect themselves, it's not their fault, and it's important to tell to stop further abuse.

Furthermore, teaching the sexual harassment unit before introducing the abduction unit can be beneficial as well because the assertiveness skills stressed in Unit 2 can be used to reinforce personal safety skills. Being able to be assertive can be especially helpful when someone a child knows asks them to do something that is against the rules such as opening the door to their home, or getting in the car, and when a friend pressures them to do something that is unsafe.

Teaching Guidelines

Administrators: Prior to implementing the child abduction program

- Accept only original certified documents when registering a child and secure records directly from a child's last school to prevent tampering of records.

- Establish a system where parents or a designated adult is required to call if a child is sick or will be absent from school. If a child does not show up in school and the parents have not called, a call should be placed to the home as soon as possible.

- Establish a system for safely releasing a child from school. It is important to have on file the names of adults to whom a child is permitted to be released. This is especially important in situations when a non-custodial parent tries to pick up a child without permission or the authority to do so. Require written parental notification if a child may be picked up by an adult, other than those listed on the form. If the person is not known to the school authorities, ask for identification.

- Provide adequate supervision during dismissal and recess time and be aware of any unauthorized person lingering around school property.

- If children remain after school for any reason make sure they have a safe, supervised way home.

Teachers/Presenters: Prior to implementing the program

- Report concerns to the building principal anytime a child appears confused about his or her name, age, last residence, family background.

- Use the classroom activities that ask parents to develop home safety plans with their children. Adult involvement is an important part of the abduction prevention program because children need to apply what they learn to their own home environment to be safe.

- Be alert to situations involving young children who reveal they are left home alone and when older elementary school age children reveal they have the responsibility to care for their younger siblings alone. Leaving a child home alone younger than 10 years old is not advisable. The maturity level of the individual child should be considered. Some parents begin to leave a child home alone for short periods of time sometimes around fourth and more often fifth grade. Children left for long periods of time or at a young age may indicate a family burdened with financial problems and few resources to provide adult supervision — and in some cases neglect. Refer concerns to an administrator or support staff in your school.

Additional Resources

The information found in the child sexual abuse prevention unit is also a useful resource here. The following agencies have a great deal of additional resource information on child safety and provide assistance in locating missing children:

■ National Center for Missing and Exploited Children, 2101 Wilson Blvd., Suite 550, Arlington, VA 22201-3052, (800) THE-LOST, http://www.missingkids.org

■ Child Find of America, Inc., 7 Innis Ave., P.O. Box 277, New Paltz, NY 12561-0277. (800) I-AM-LOST, (914) 255-1848.

Resources

Abduction Prevention Children's Books, Curricula and Educator's Resources

ABCs of Health and Safety: A Written-in-Rhyme Coloring Book. Flushing, N.Y.: Promotional Slideguide, 1996. (718) 886-8408. Health and safety tips accompany every letter from A to Z. Topics include protecting your skin from the sun, the basics of good nutrition, personal well-being, safety at home and safety in the neighborhood.

Berenstein, Jan and Stan. *The Berenstein Bears Learn about Strangers.* New York: Random House, 1985. Story book for younger children about never talking to a stranger, never accepting presents from a stranger, and never ever going anywhere with a stranger.

Be Smart, Dial 9-1-1 Coloring and Activities Book. Flushing, N.Y.: Promotional Slideguide, 1996. (718) 886-8408. This book teaches children how to call and what to say in an emergency whether at home or at an outdoor phone. It advises to call 911 if there's a fire, if you swallow poison, if you're home alone and frightened, or if a friend gets hurt while playing.

Be Smart, Say No to Strangers: An Educational Coloring and Activities Book. Flushing, N.Y.: Promotional Slideguide, 1996. (718) 886-8408. Topics include how to avoid "tricks" strangers might use, what to do (and not to do) in the street, in stores and at home alone, good *v.* bad touching, phone smarts, and how to use 911. It also includes people to talk to if a child needs help.

Child Find Coloring Books: Color me Safe; Shopping is Fun; Safety Club; and *What-if . . . .* Child Find of America, P.O. Box 277, New Paltz, N.Y., 12561. These coloring books are excellent materials for both classroom use and to send home with students for parent/child reinforcement of safety awareness.

Child Safety on the Information Highway. Arlington, Va.: National Center for Missing and Exploited Children, 1994. A brochure about the risks for children on the internet, how parents can reduce the risks, and guidelines for parents.

Girard, Linda. *Who is a Stranger and What Should I Do?* Niles, Ill.: Alberty Whitman & Co., 1985. This book focuses on strangers, who they are and what to do about them in many different circumstances. It also includes questions to ask parents or teachers and practice situations, which both initiate helpful discussions.

Kids and Company Teacher's Guide: A Comprehensive Manual for Grades K-5/6. Arlington, Va.: The National Center for Missing and Exploited Children and the Adam Walsh Children's Fund, 1988. 1-800-892-7430. A curriculum of activities presented for different grade levels and a resource manual for educators.

Kraizer, Sherryll. *The Safe Child Book: A Common Sense Approach to Protecting Children and Teaching Children to Protect Themselves.* New York: Simon and Schuster, 1996. Excellent resource for educators and parents. Covers all aspects of protecting children and includes a good section on abduction prevention and internet safety.

Let's Learn About Home Safety: An Educational Coloring and Activities Book. Flushing, N.Y.: Promotional Slideguide, 1996. (718) 886-8408. Topics include the dangers of playing with matches, keeping the front door shut to strangers, staying away from hazardous materials, and how to dial 9-1-1 in an emergency.

McGruff, Safe Kids Identification Kit: A Fun Way to Family Safety. Plainview, N.Y.: The Bureau for At-Risk Youth, 1-800-99-YOUTH. Includes a 10-page book to teach kids how to respond to a variety of situations, easy-to-use fingerprint and identification section, a Safe Kid Card and suggestions for parents.

Make-My-Own-Book Kit: I Say No to Strangers. Plainview, N.Y.: The Bureau For At-Risk Youth. 1-800-99-YOUTH. This easy "All By Myself" activity project allows kids to color, cut, paste, trace, and lace while learning what they can and cannot do, including not going for a ride with a stranger but able to take candy from their parents. Suggested for ages 3-7.

Safety Flash Cards. Syosset, N.Y.: Playing it Safe. 1-800-PLAY-IT-SAFE. These flash cards teach children how to safely react to situations they may encounter. The card has a safety scene on one side and a statement and questions about the safest thing to do on the other side.

Silverman Saunders, Carol. *Safe at School Awareness and Action for Parents of Kids Grades K-12.* Minneapolis, Minn.: Free Spirit Publishing, 1994. This book covers all aspects of school safety for parents and school to work on together.

Timmy's ABCs of Personal Safety: An Educational Coloring and Activities Book. Flushing, N.Y.: Promotional Slideguide, 1996. (718) 886-8408. In this book, Timmy the Dinosaur takes a tour of the ABCs to help kids master personal safety. It begins with "A is for Aware" (Be aware of everything around you. That will help to protect you from getting hurt), concludes with "Z is for Zone" (Help keep your school and neighborhood a drug-free, smoke-free, and gang-free zone) and covers a great deal of other topics in between.

Wagner, Jan. *Raising Kids in an Unsafe World: 30 Simple Ways to Prevent Your Child From Being Lost, Abducted, or Abused.* New York: Avon Books, 1996. Provides good background information for both educators and parents.

Watson, Carol. *Run, Yell, and Tell: A Safety Book for Children.* Minneapolis: Missing Children Minnesota, 1993. A storybook appropriate for young children, including some activities and a song, that tells about a young child who learns about abduction prevention in school.

Abudction Prevention Videos

McGruff on Dangerous Strangers. AIMS Multimedia, 9710 DeSoto Ave., Chatsworth, CA 91311. VHS 1/2" cassette, 15 minutes. (800) 367-2467. McGruff, the crime dog, reviews practical ways children can stay safe on the way home from school as well as in other locations and situations.

Nick News: Stranger Danger. Lucky Duck Productions. Available only for free rental in most Blockbuster Video stores nationwide. An excellent video that includes role plays by students to show the safe thing to do when in public to avoid stranger abduction. Suggested for grades 4–6.

Stranger Safety: The Safety Adventure of Eli Sprightly. The Bureau for At-Risk Youth, 645 New York Ave., Huntington, NY 11743. VHS 1/2" cassette, 14 minutes. (800) 99-YOUTH. Uses scenarios that present common stranger situations. Suggested for grades 2–4.

Staying Home Alone. AIMS Multimedia, 9710 DeSoto Ave., Chatsworth, CA 91311. VHS 1/2" cassette, 15 minutes. (800) 367-2467. Shows dramatization that teach children how to stay safe and handle a variety of situations when home alone.

Too Smart for Strangers. Distributed by Movies Unlimited, 3015 Darnell Rd., Philadelphia, PA 19154. (800) 466-8437. Uses Winnie the Pooh characters to teach about safety rules to prevent abduction by strangers. Also reinforces the concepts of good and bad touches, saying no, and telling. Suggested for grades K–3.

Unit 3: Child Abduction Prevention

Part B: Classroom Materials

Abduction Prevention Curriculum for Grades K-3

Goals

- Students will learn to recognize dangerous situations that could put them at risk for abduction both at home and away from home.

- Students will learn prevention strategies (what never to do) to avoid being an easy target for abduction.

- Students will learn personal safety rules to help keep them safe at home and when away from home.

- Students will learn how to safely get help if they are lost or in case of an emergency.

Introduce Topic

Explain: We have learned about lots of ways to help children be safe. We learned about being safe at home and at school. We have also learned that no one has a right to touch you in ways that make you feel uncomfortable or treat you in ways that make you feel bad or unsafe.

You also have a right to be safe from dangerous people who try to take children and hurt them. That's why grownups always say never to talk to strangers. They want to make sure you are safe from people who may want to harm you.

It is important for you to know this doesn't happen to most kids. In fact, because it happens to very few children in the whole country, kids really don't have to worry about this happening to them most of the time.

However, sometimes when kids hear in the news about scary things like a child who gets taken or a child who is missing (abducted or kidnapped) they may feel afraid especially if they haven't learned what to do to keep themselves safe. A child might think that can happen to me, "I play in the playground or I walk home from school."

You are going to learn about the different kinds of situations where you need to be careful. You will also learn how to keep yourself safe from danger so you don't have to feel afraid. Instead you can say, "I know what to watch out for," "I know how to stay away from danger," and "I know how to keep myself safe." Knowing what to do helps you to be safe and feel safe.

Classroom Activities

1. **The Safe Thing to Do.** This activity uses a game format and role plays to give students an opportunity to practice the safe thing to do near a car, in a store, on a neighborhood street, and in the house.

Part B: Classroom Materials

145

2. **Family Safety Plan.** A family safety plan worksheet is provided for younger students to bring home to complete with a parent or adult in charge. The completed plan is then reviewed and reinforced in class.

Activity 1 — The Safe Thing To Do

Explain

Even though you are not old enough to be home alone or out in public places without a grownup, kids your age could be in a situation where you will need to know the safe thing to do to stay away from danger. For example, you need to know the safe thing to do when you are playing near your home and a stranger approaches you and asks for help to find a lost pet. You need to know the safe thing to do if you get separated from your parents in a store and need help finding them. You need to know the safe thing to do when you answer the door or phone at home when an adult is not available.

You also will need to know the safe thing to do with all kinds of people. You need to know the safe thing to do with a stranger. And you need to know what to do when the person is someone familiar but you don't know well. You may know their name or have seen them around, and they may even know your name, such as a local store owner, a person who lives down the block, or your sister's friend. You even need to know how to stay safe with people you know well.

Someone is not a "safe person" to be alone with when that person is:

■ a stranger — it is never safe to be alone with someone you do not know or know well even if they seem nice and look OK. If you are by yourself in public, even if you are surrounded by lots of people, and a stranger tries to be friendly and have a conversation with you, it is not safe. Strangers who may be dangerous often try to become a child's friend before trying to get a child to go somewhere alone with them.

■ anyone who touches you in a way that makes you feel uncomfortable — get away from that person as fast as you can whether he or she is a stranger or someone you know well.

■ anyone who tries to trick you into going somewhere alone with them by saying "follow me," "come with me," or "get in the car" — these are tricks used by dangerous people. Never trust someone who tries to trick you into going with them.

■ anyone who says, "It's OK not to follow your parents' rules, it will be our secret" — anytime someone asks you to keep a secret or to promise not to tell your parents about something that happened or something they want you to do, something is wrong. Adults who are safe to be around will say instead, "I understand you have rules about opening the door, accepting a ride, or going with someone. I will wait for you to get permission first.

- anyone your parents have not given you permissiuon to go with or be alone with who says it's OK to go with them anyway — this is an unsafe person to go anywhere with. Adults who are safe to be around will say instead, "You are right to ask first. That's the safe thing to do.

- anyone who makes you feel, "Uh-oh. This doesn't feel right," — anytime someone makes you feel uncomfortable, that is a person who is not safe for you to be alone with.

Activity

Set up four "safe-thing-to-do" stations. These can be as simple as a poster taped to a desk or as elaborate as a large oak tag cut-out propped on a desktop. Four desks will represent different situations children need to practice the safe thing to do and should include: #1 car, #2 store, #3 neighborhood street, #4 house.

There are 11 safe-thing-to-do what-if situations provided for this activity. Divide the class up so that every child gets a turn to participate once. Depending on the size of the class two or more children may be asked to act out the same situation. Repeating a situation and having different kids act out the same thing provides an excellent opportunity for reinforcing the safety rules.

Make copies of the what-if situations and cut them up so that all the #1 situations involving a car are placed on the desk with the car on it, all the situations involving a store on the #2 desk, the situations involving the neighborhood street on #3 desk, and the situations on the house the #4 desk.

The teacher should circulate to each desk and invite the students up one by one until all the situations are role played and every student has a turn.

Before each role play the teacher should present the what-if situation and the safety rules that apply. The safety rules become the guidelines for what the child should act out in front of the class.

Then the teacher should role play the person trying to trick the child and the student should be instructed to act out the safe thing to do for that situation based on the safety rules presented. The goal here is to have the child show the rest of the class the safe thing to do while practicing the skills needed to protect themselves.

The Safe-Thing-to-Do What-If Situations

#1 Car What-If:

You are in the playground and your mom is not sitting near where you are playing with a ball. Your ball rolls near the street. A man in a van pulls up and asks you for help to find his lost puppy. He wants to show you a picture of his puppy and asks you to come close to the car.

Before the role play the teacher should explain: When a stranger in a car tries to get you to come near the car by asking for help to find a lost animal it's a dangerous trick and you should:

- Never go near a car that stops for help or directions. Stay at least three large steps back from the car.
- Run in the opposite direction the car is facing.
- Never agree to help an adult. Adults should ask adults for help.
- Immediately tell a grownup in charge about the person who tried to trick you.

> **Teacher:** Role play the man in the van.
>
> **Student:** Role play the safe thing to do when a stranger calls you near the car and asks for help.

#1 Car What-if:

You are supposed to meet your best friend with her mom and walk together to the playground after school. You wait and wait but they don't show up. The playground is only a block away. You decide to see if they are waiting there for you. As you are walking alone to the playground a car pulls up next to you. A lady you don't know says, "You're (use student's name) _____ right? Your mom said you would be wearing a T-shirt with your name on it and I would recognize you. Your mom had an accident and is in the hospital. Get in the car. Your mom said I should pick you up and take you there."

Before the role play the teacher should explain: When a stranger tells you to get in their car by saying there's been an emergency or someone is sick it is a dangerous trick and you should:

- Stay at least three large steps back from the car.
- Always ask for the code word that you and your parents made up that means it's OK to go with the person who knows the code.
- If the person does not know the code word do not get in the car or go anywhere with that person.
- Run in the opposite direction the car is facing. Go to where people are and get help.
- Never go places alone. Its always safer to go with a friend or an adult.
- Never wear your name on a T-shirt or book bag. Someone can try to trick you by making believe they know you just because they know your name.

> **Teacher:** Role play the lady in the car.
>
> **Student:** Role play the safe thing to do if someone says this an emergency and I am supposed to pick you up.

#1 Car What-if:

You are walking to school with your older brother and his friends. It starts raining really hard. Someone you recognize from the neighborhood who you and your parents do not know well pulls up and says, "You kids are getting drenched. I am going in the direction of your school. Get in I will give you a ride." When the kids hesitate he says, "It's OK to come with me. I live in the neighborhood and know your parents. They won't mind."

Before the role play the teacher should explain:

■ Never accept a ride with someone you don't know or know well if you don't have permission first.

■ Any adult who your parents have not given you permission to go with who says its OK to go with them anyway is not a safe person to go with.

■ Adults who are safe to be around will say instead, "You are right to ask first. That's the safe thing to do."

Teacher: Role play the adult offering the kids a ride to school.

Student: Role play to safe thing to do when someone you do not know well offers you a ride.

#2 Store What-if:

You are in the department store with your mom. You wander away from your mom's side for a minute to check out a cool game nearby. When you look back up she's gone. You look all over the store and yell, "Mom, Mom," but she doesn't answer. A man comes up to you and asks if you are lost. He says he saw someone looking for a child just like you. He says he works for the store and you should come with him. He takes your hand and starts leading you away.

Before the role play the teacher should explain:

■ When a stranger tries to get you to follow them when you are lost, it is a dangerous trick.

■ Run away from this person and go to someone who you know really works in the store because they are behind the counter or cash register.

■ If someone tries to touch you or take your hand and lead you somewhere yell, "This is not my father. This is not my mother. Help, Help."

■ If you are lost don't wander around the store yourself looking for your parent(s). Get help from someone who works in the store near the place where you last remember being with your parent.

Teacher: Role play the man in the store.

Student: Role play the safe thing to do if you are lost and someone says follow me.

#2 Store What-if

You and your dad are in the store and your dad is waiting on line to buy something. You are nearby looking at comic books. A lady comes over to you and says she is giving away free comic books right outside the store. You say you have to wait for your dad. She tells you that it will only take a second and if you hurry up and come with her you can get some before they are all gone.

Before the role play the teacher should explain:

- If someone tries to get you to follow them by offering free stuff, presents, or money this is a dangerous trick.
- Get away as fast as you can when someone tries to trick you into going with them.
- Never go anywhere with someone you don't know.
- Never take money, presents, or anything from someone you don't know or know well.
- Always ask first before going anywhere with someone or before taking anything from someone.
- Always tell a grownup about a dangerous person who tries to trick you.

Teacher: Role play the lady in the store.

Student: Role play the safe thing to do if someone offers you a free present and says come with me to get it.

#3 Neighborhood What-if

You are playing basketball with your friend in your neighbor's front yard. Your friend's mom calls him in for dinner. You decide to stay and shoot a few more baskets before you go home. A man you don't know says, "I have been watching you play ball. My own little boy is home sick and can't play ball. Maybe I could bring him over to watch sometime. Is this where you live? My name is Mr. Smith. My little boy's name is John. What's your name?"

Before the role play the teacher should explain:

- Always play outside with a friend and stay with your friend when you are away from home and out in public.
- Do not play alone or go places alone when you are away from home or in public.
- Don't talk to a stranger or someone you don't know well when you are alone and somewhere without an adult.
- Never give your name, phone number, or your address to someone you don't know or know well.

Teacher: Role play the stranger in the yard.

Student: Role play the safe thing to do if a stranger acts friendly, talks to you and wants to know your name and where you live.

#3 Neighborhood What-if:

You are playing in your yard with two friends. A man comes over and asks you and your friends for help to find his lost kitten. He says his little girl will be heartbroken if he doesn't find it. He will give one dollar to anyone who helps. He says, "Follow me I will show you where I last saw the kitten so you will know where to look."

Before the role play the teacher should explain:

- If someone tries to get you to follow them by saying their pet is lost and needs help, this is a dangerous trick.
- Never take money from someone you don't know or don't know well.
- Always ask first before you take anything from anyone.
- Never agree to help an adult. Adults should ask other adults for help, not children.
- Never go anywhere with someone you don't know or know well.
- Always ask first before going anywhere with anyone.

Teacher: Role play the man in the yard.

Student: Role play the safe thing to do if an adult asks for help and offers you money.

#4 Home What-if:

Your dad is busy working on his car when the phone rings. He asks you to get it. It is a man asking for someone you never heard of. You say, "You have the wrong number." The other person asks, "What number did I get?"

Before the role play the teacher should explain: Never give your phone number, your address, or name over the phone to someone you don't know or don't know well.

Teacher: Role play the man on the phone.

Student: Role play the safe thing to do if an adult asks for your phone number on the phone.

#4 Home What-if:

Your mom is upstairs taking a rest. The door bell rings. It is a delivery man who says he has a package to deliver for your mom. You tell him your mom can't come to the door right now. You ask him to please leave the package at the door. He says, "Someone has to sign for the package. I can't leave the package if you don't open he door and sign for it. Your mom won't get her package then."

Before the role play the teacher should explain: Even if you are not home alone, if you are the person answering the door, never open the door for a stranger or someone you don't know well without permission first.

Teacher: Role play the delivery man.

Student: Role play the safe thing to do if an adult tries to get you to open he door.

#4 Home What-if:

Your older brother promised to buy bread for dinner and forgot. You were in the middle of your favorite show and you begged to stay home alone. He said he would be gone only a few minutes and it would be OK just this once. After he left, the door bell rang. When you asked who it was a man said there was an accident and he needed to call an ambulance. He asked to come in and use the phone. You say your mom can't come to the door right now and you can't open the door without her permission. The man asks if you are alone and afraid to open the door. He then says its OK because this is an emergency.

Before the role play the teacher should explain:

- Never open the door for a stranger or someone you don't know well without permission even if the person says its an emergency.
- Never tell anyone you are home alone.
- Call your mom or dad or another adult and ask them for help.

Teacher: Role play the man at the door.

Student: Role play the safe thing to do if an adult tries to get you to open the door.

#4 Home What-if:

Your dad is working in his office at home. He says he needs to finish something important and doesn't want to be disturbed. The phone rings. Someone says, "This is a delivery person. Can I please speak to your mom or dad?" When you say they can't come to the phone right now, the person says, "That's OK I just need to check your name and address so I can deliver the package. What is your name and address?"

Before the role play the teacher should explain:

- Never give your name, address, or phone number to someone over the phone or to someone you meet in person.
- Tell your parent about the phone call.

Teacher: Role play the delivery man on the phone.

Student: Role play the safe thing to do if an adult tries to get you to give your name and address on the phone.

Activity 2 — Family Safety Plan

Parents need to encourage personal safety discussions in the home to facilitate the practical application of safe habits as part of daily family life. For this purpose a Family Safety Plan worksheet (Handout #1) is provided for younger students to bring home to complete with a parent. This is an important part of the abduction prevention program. It provides an opportunity to enable parents to reinforce the prevention concepts and gives them some insight into the material covered.

Explain to the students that for homework they are being asked to work on a Family Safety Plan with an adult or parent at home. This is because an important part of being safe is learning about the rules in your own home that can help you be safe.

After the students bring their completed family safety plan back to class review their answers with each child. Make sure each student has learned their full name, address, and phone number. Some children may need to practice this for a period of time with a parent at home.

Once the children have learned to communicate their name, address, and phone number bring in a phone to class and have the students practice calling 911. Explain that an important part of being safe is knowing how to get help in case of an emergency.

The following coloring books, annotated in the bibliography, are excellent reinforcement materials for classroom use/or sending home with students to promote parent/child reinforcement of safety awareness: *Color Me Safe, Shopping is Fun, Safety Club,* and *What-if* . . . (see Unit 3A, Resources).

Handout #1
Family Safety Plan

Dear Parent(s),

Your child is participating in an abduction prevention program to learn child safety protection skills. This program teaches children never to go anywhere with anyone, get in a car with anyone, open the door for anyone, or give out personal information in person or on the phone to anyone without a parent's permission first. The following is a safety checklist to review with your child to make sure your child knows what to do to be safe at home and away from home.

1) Children need to know who in your neighborhood is safe to go to for help. This is especially important if your child has reached an age to play outside without adult supervision.

   Have your child list three people in your neighborhood it is Ok to go to for help:

   ■ _____

   ■ _____

   ■ _____

2) Your child should never go anywhere with anyone unless they have permission to go with that person. Make up a secret code word with your child. If you send someone to pick up your child and they know the secret code word then it is safe to go. If someone tries to get your child to go with them and the person does not know the secret code word, then your child will know its not safe to go with that person.

   ☐ I know my secret code word and won't go anywhere with someone unless they know it too.

3) It is not safe for a child to go places alone or play outside alone. Children should be encouraged to use the buddy system.

   ☐ I talked to my family about not going places alone and staying with my friends whenever we go places together.

   List at least three friends or buddies you could safely go places with:

   ■ _____

   ■ _____

   ■ _____

4) Your child should not openly display their name on clothing or possessions. It is easier to trick a child into thinking a stranger is someone the child knows and is safe to talk to just because they know the child's name.

☐ I checked my clothing and possessions and made sure my name is not on the outside for strangers to see.

5) It is important for your child to know identifying information and how to call 911 to enable them to get help in case they are lost, they are in danger, or there is an emergency. Make sure your child knows the following information about themselves. Keep practicing until they know it well:

Name _____

Address (including town or city and state) _____

_____

Phone number (including area code) _____

Practice with your child calling 911 with a phone that is unplugged. Have your child give his name, address, phone number, and the reason for the call. Instruct your child not to hang up until the operator tells you to.

6) Having clear-cut safety rules for your child to follow can help reduce a child's vulnerability. When a child knows the rules it can give a child the confidence to say, "No. I am not allowed to do that or go with you without permission. Its against my parents' rules."

My safety rules are:
☐ I will ask permission before getting in a car with anyone.
☐ I will ask permission before going anywhere with anyone even if its with someone I know.
☐ I will ask permission before taking anything from anyone.
☐ I will stay far away from a stranger in a car who asks for help or directions.
☐ I will never open the door at home without permission first.
☐ I know my secret code word and won't go anywhere with someone unless they know it too.
☐ I will not go places alone and will stay with my friends whenever we go places together.
☐ I will not give my name, address, or phone number to someone I do not know or know well on the phone, in person, or on the internet.
☐ I will never tell anyone if I am home alone.

☐ I will tell a grownup and get help if someone touches me in a way that makes me feel uncomfortable, asks me to keep a secret from my parents, tells me not to follow my safety rules, tries to get me to go somewhere, or do something I do not have permission to do.

7) Make a list of emergency numbers to post by the phone that includes:

☐ your address and phone number

☐ mom's work number

☐ dad's work number

☐ name and number of doctor

☐ name and number of several contact people to call if mom or dad can't be reached

☐ 911 and/or police, fire department numbers

Abduction Prevention
Curriculum for Grades 4-6

Goals

- Students will learn to recognize dangerous situations that could put them at risk for abduction both at home and away from home.

- Students will learn prevention strategies (what never to do) to avoid being an easy target for abduction.

- Students will learn personal safety rules that will help keep them safe at home and when away from home.

- Students will learn how to safely get help if they are lost or in case of an emergency.

Introduce Topic

Explain: We have learned lots of ways to help children be safe. We learned about being safe at home and at school and that no one has a right to touch you in ways that make you feel uncomfortable or treat you in ways that make you feel bad or unsafe.

You also have a right to be safe from dangerous people who try to take children and hurt them. That's why grownups always say never to talk to strangers. They want to make sure you are safe from people who may want to harm you.

It is important for you to know this doesn't happen to most kids. In fact, because it happens to very few children in the whole country, kids really don't have to worry about this happening to them most of the time.

However, sometimes when kids hear in the news about scary things like a child who gets taken or a child who is missing (abducted or kidnapped) they may feel afraid especially if they haven't learned what to do to keep themselves safe. A child may think that can happen to me, "I play in the playground or I walk home from school."

You are going to learn about the different kinds of situations where you need to be careful. You will also learn how to keep yourself safe from danger so you don't have to feel afraid. Instead you can say, "I know what to watch out for to stay away from danger," and "I know how to keep myself safe." Knowing what to do will help you be safe and feel safe.

Classroom Activities

3. **On Your Own and Safe.** This activity provides stories and discussion questions about kids who were out on their own and had to take responsibility for their own safety. It teaches the safe thing to do when out in public on your own with all different kinds of people.

4. **What Kids Need to Know to Stay Away from Danger.** This activity explains what to look for if someone is not a safe person to be alone with. It provides what-if situations and a safety check list for students to consider when discussing the situations.

5. **Playing it Safe When Home Alone.** This activity teaches older kids who may be home alone with safe things to do before you enter an empty house, how to answer the door and phone safely, how to be safe on the internet, and how to handle an emergency. Students are then asked to complete a home alone and safety plan with their parents.

Activity 3 — On Your Own and Safe

Explain

Most abductions occur close to home in a public place or on the street such as at a shopping mall, a playground, walking home from school, playing in the neighborhood, or the video arcade.

Because you are older now and have more freedom to be out in public without a grownup you need to know how to be responsible for your own safety. When you were little, grownups made sure you were safe. Now it's up to you.

When you are in public on your own you may have a chance to see and meet lots of different kinds of people. This means you need to know the safe thing to do in all kinds of situations and with all kinds of people not only with strangers or someone you don't at all.

You will also need to know the safe thing to do when the person is someone familiar to you but you don't know well. You may know their name or have seen them around. They may even know your name, such as a local store owner, a person who lives down the block, or your sister's friend. You also need to know what to do if someone you know asks you to do something that is unsafe.

We are going to read stories about kids who had to learn the hard way about the importance of taking responsibility for their own safety.

Read the stories "Short Cut," "Super Safe," and "Girlfriends" [*]

- Discussion questions and reinforcement concepts follow for each story. First process these with the class as a whole.

- Then use a small group format by breaking the class into three groups and assign each group one of the stories to work with. Give each group a safety checklist, Handout #1, that identifies the dangerous things to watch out for, unsafe things never to do, and safety rules. For each situation have

---

[*]"Short Cut," "Super Safe," and "Girlfriends" are adapted from Oralee Wachtler, *Close to Home*. Reprinted by permission of Scholastic, Inc.

158

the students decide which items on the checklist apply to their story. Have each group take turns to present their findings to the class.

"Girlfriends"

Gina and Kim were in the sixth grade and best friends. They lived at the top of Hillcrest Road, the steepest, longest hill in the whole city. Every day since first grade they had walked home together all seven blocks to the top.

Halfway up the hill Gina and Kim turned around and walked backward to give their tired legs a rest. It gave them a clear view of any car that was coming up the hill. When they saw someone they knew like a neighbor or one of Kim's brothers, Gina would stick out her thumb and beg for a ride to the top of the hill. Sometimes it worked.

Gina noticed a blue car climbing slowly up the hill, getting closer and closer. "Here comes a car," said Gina. "I want a ride."

"Is it someone we know?" asked Kim hopefully.

When the car finally made it up to them, it stopped, and the young man wearing a T-shirt waved to them. He stuck his head out the window and called to them. "Hi," he said. "Do you girls know where Mountain View Road is?"

"Sure. It's two more blocks straight up the hill," Gina told him.

"Great. Thanks a lot. Are you going that way?" he asked.

"Yeah. We go all the way to the top," said Gina. "Well then, get in, and I'll drive you," said the man.

"No. That's okay," said Kim. "We can walk."

Gina looked at Kim. "C'mon, let's get in. I will if you will," she said.

"You go ahead if you want to," said Kim. "I'm walking."

"I guess I'll walk," Gina said to him.

"Okay. Whatever you say. Maybe I'll see you around again some time." He waved as he drove up the hill. Gina waved back.

"Why'd you say no?" complained Gina. "Now we have to walk up this humongous hill."

"Didn't you ever hear about not talking to strangers?" said Kim.

"He wasn't that kind of stranger. He wasn't a weirdo or anything," said Gina.

"What if he didn't want to let us out of the car? Then what?"

"Well, you didn't have to be so mean to him," said Gina.

"You didn't have to be so nice to him, either," said Kim. "He was some man I don't even know who tried to pick up two girls. He gave me a creepy feeling."

"He wasn't a man. He wasn't any older than your brother," said Gina."I think he was cute."

159

"You would," said Kim. "You act like such a baby sometimes," said Gina. "I wish you'd just grow up." Kim didn't answer. They walked silently to the top of the hill and parted.

The next day Kim was still mad. She started up the hill alone. It seemed longer and steeper without someone to talk to. Even arguing with Gina is better than this , she thought. Then she saw the same blue car parked up ahead.

"Hi, remember me?" Kim ignored him. "Want a ride?" he asked.

"No," she answered. Kim crossed the street to get away from him. She turned around and walked backward to see what he was going to do next. Just then Kim saw Gina walking up the hill toward the blue car. She wondered if Gina would be dumb enough to get in the car with him. Then she saw the man put his hand on Gina's shoulder. It gave Kim that creepy feeling about him again. She started to run down the hill at full speed toward Gina.

"What do you want?" said Gina. "What's wrong?"

"C'mon, Gina," said the man. "Let's go." He kept his hand on Gina's shoulder and pulled her closer to him. Kim grabbed Gina's other arm.

"Don't, Gina. We're walking." Gina looked at Kim.

"I guess I'd better not," Gina said to the man.

"C'mon," said Kim. "Let's just go home Gina, please."

"Don't listen to her. She's just a kid," he said to Gina. "Let's go." He took her arm and tried to pull her into the car.

Kim started yelling, "Let go of her, leave us alone. I told my father about you. I took the license number. He's going to report you to the police. You better get out of here."

With that he let go of Gina. Kim and Gina ran as fast as they could in the other direction. When they were far enough away, they stopped to catch their breath.

Gina said, "Do you think he was trying to kidnap me or something?"

"Yup or I wouldn't have gotten his license number for my mom. I know she'll call the police and have them check the guy out. I sure don't want him getting a hold of us — or any other kids for that matter."

"Girlfriends" Discussion Questions:

■ Should Gina and Kim have hitchhiked with people they knew in the first place?

■ Kim said to Gina "You go if you want to." Is that a good idea? Why or why not?

■ Gina thought that the guy driving the car wasn't the kind of stranger you had to worry about. Do you think you can tell whether a stranger is someone you can trust by how they look? What else do you need to watch out for to be safe?

- Gina tried to pressure Kim to get in the car with her. How hard is it to listen to your feelings when you are being pressured by a friend to do something that is unsafe or makes you feel uncomfortable? Would it be important enough to get mad at your friend over? Why or why not?

Reinforce

- You should never accept a ride with anyone, even with someone you know without checking it out first with your parents. When this is something you do automatically then you don't even have to try to figure out "does this person seem OK or not or is it a safe thing to do or not." It just becomes a habit and something you do to keep yourself safe.

- If a stranger in a car tries to get you to come near the car by offering you a ride, asking you for directions, or help to find a lost animal stay at least three large steps back from the car and if necessary run in the opposite direction the car is facing.

- Trying to do the safe thing all the time can also help you stand up to a friend or even an adult who is trying to pressure you to do something that makes you feel uncomfortable or that is against your family rules. Just because you know it is the right thing to do can help you speak up firmly and refuse to go along with them.

- Remember we learned that confusing touches by someone you know and like can make you feel "Uh-oh, this doesn't feel right" and that you should trust your feelings and say no and get away. That "Uh-oh" feeling can help you out here as well. Listen to your feelings whenever someone does something that makes you feel "Uh-oh. This doesn't feel right." This will help you do the safe thing for yourself or a friend.

"Super Safe"

Janie's mother worked at home in her office upstairs. She had a sign on the door that said Do Not Disturb Unless It Is Really Important. Janie walked her mom to her office.

"Bye, Mom," said Janie. "Have a good day at the office."

"I will. Remember the rules?" asked her mother

"Number one, no interruptions, unless it's super important. Number two, don't go anywhere without asking first. And number three, Pam's in charge," answered Janie.

"Right," said her mom. "If I finish my work early, I'll meet you and Pam at the playground." Pam was Janie's baby sitter.

Janie's mom left a shopping list for Janie and Pam.

Just as they were about to leave, the doorbell rang. It was Pam's boyfriend, Gary. He came over to show Pam his new truck. "Want to go for a ride in my new pickup?" he asked. "I'll take you both for a ride around the block."

"We have to go to the store," said Pam, "and then to the playground."

"I'll drive you. Come on. It's a great car. You'll love it," said Gary.

Janie wanted to go but she wasn't sure if it was OK. "Let's go ask Mom," she said.

"No, we're not supposed to interrupt. Remember?" answered Pam. "Gary's a friend of mine. I'm sure she won't mind. Let's go."

The three of them sat up front and Gary drove them to the beach, past the store, and the playground.

When Janie's mom got to the playgound after work Janie and Pam were nowhere to be found. Janie's mother began to worry about all the kinds of things that might have happened. She called the hospital and was about to call the police department when Janie and Pam walked in carrying groceries.

"Hi, Mom," said Janie. "We went for a ride in Gary's new truck."

Janie's mom was glad they were home safe but she looked serious and said, "Who's Gary? Who gave you permission to get into a truck? Why didn't you go to the playgound like you were supposed to?" she asked all at once.

Pam tried to explain. "I guess it was my fault," she said. "Gary's a friend of mine. I thought it would be OK because I know him really well."

"But I don't know him," said Janie's mom. "And that's the point. You're not allowed to go anywhere with a person I don't know. It's as simple as that. Always ask me first. Don't go anywhere without my permission. That's a rule. I have to know where Janie is and who she is with all the time. You have to follow the rules so I know you're safe — super safe — even when I'm not with you."

"Super Safe" Discussion Questions

- Why are the rules Janie's mom talked about important?
- Even though Janie knew the rules about asking for permission why did she listen to Pam anyway and not bother asking her mom.
- If Gary is a friend of Pam's does that make it OK for Janie to go in his car? Why or why not?
- What if Gary was someone Janie knew well such as her sister's boyfriend would it be OK to go in his car then?
- What could Janie say to Pam to assert herself and make sure she does the right thing?
- Why was Janie's mom upset and worried?
- What if Janie wanted to call first and check it out? What if her mom was not available, what should she do?

Reinforce

■ Sometimes kids think they are supposed to listen to someone else even when they know its wrong and against the rules just because someone older said so. It is always OK to say no and assert yourself in order to be safe even with adults or someone in charge. Also emphasize that the safest thing to do is not to go in a car or go anywhere with someone you don't have permission to go with even if you know the person well.

■ Trust your feelings. If your feelings are telling you that something doesn't feel right then don't do it even if an adult or someone in charge tells you it is OK to do.

■ Kids often think that if they are introduced to someone or the person they meet knows someone in their family or their friend that this new acquaintance is not a stranger and safe to be with. This is not true. Someone you just met, or someone you see in your neighborhood and don't really know well is not someone you or your parents know well enough for you to be alone with or in their car.

■ As you get older and more independent you may not feel like asking permission if you are old enough to do certain things. Checking with an adult to make sure if its the safe thing to do is not the same as asking if you are allowed to do something. Checking whether it is safe to get in a car, let someone into your home, or go with someone could help you avoid serious danger. That's why it is important to have someone else to contact just in case your parents or guardian can't be reached to ask.

"Shortcut"

Paul was late for school again. Everyone was already in the classroom when he entered. Mrs. Schaffer, his teacher, looked up from her desk when Paul opened the door. "Late again," she said. "We'll talk about it after school, now just get to work."

"I can't stay today. I have hockey practice after school," said Paul. "Coach is choosing the team to play in the league. If I am late again he'll drop me."

Mrs. Schaffer was not impressed. "We'll talk about it after school."

At three o'clock the bell rang. Paul watched his friends go off to hockey practice with their sticks and skates. At three-thirty she finally let him go, and Paul dashed out the door. If he wasn't on the ice by four o'clock sharp, his coach would make him sit on the bench for the whole practice.

The safest way to get there was through the shopping mall then down the main street. The fastest way was to take the shortcut. Paul thought about it for a minute. The shortcut was through a vacant lot full of weeds and bushes and junk. Nobody was supposed to go in. There was a fence around it to keep people out, but someone had cut through the fence and made an opening.

Paul knew the shortcut was off limits. All the kids did. Sometimes Paul and his friends raced through it together anyway. Paul had never taken the shortcut by himself. The place looked kind of scary in the late afternoon shadows. He wished his friends were there. Should I or shouldn't I? he asked himself. He stepped through a hole in the fence and could see the skating rink in the distance as he started to walk through the tangled weeds. He walked a little faster, thinking about how much he wanted to make the team. Paul had gone more than halfway when a man stepped out of the bushes ahead.

"Hey, you there," the man called out. "What are you doing here?" Paul's heart was suddenly beating very fast. "You're not supposed to be here. This is private property," said the man. "Come with me." The man took a few steps toward him, getting closer and closer.

Paul wanted to run, but for a moment, he couldn't move.

"What do you mean?" said Paul. "Where are we going?"

"Stay right there," said the man. He pointed to a van parked on the other side of the field. "I'm going to take you home before you get into trouble." The man keep walking slowing toward him. He was almost close enough to touch, when he reached out to grab Paul's arm. Paul jumped back. He ducked to the side, spun around, and ran. His heart was pounding so loud he could hear it. He was afraid to look back. He kept running through the parking lot, past the stores until he reached hockey practice.

It was too late to bother putting on his uniform. At half time the coach noticed him sitting on the bench. He asked Paul what took him so long.

"Well," said Paul, "I had to stay after school 'cause I was late getting there. So I took a shortcut across that deserted lot. I knew the place wasn't safe but I did it anyway. A man came out of nowhere. He acted like a guard but he tried to grab me and put me in his van."

"What did you do?" asked the coach.

"I just took off. I ran away from him. That's why I didn't get here on time," said Paul. "This is probably the worst day of my life."

"I'd say this was your lucky day," said the coach. "You were lucky to get away. You also learned something very important today that can help you out in the future. Don't go off by yourself. Stick with your friends. Stay with the group. And keep out of places that aren't safe."

"I guess so but I didn't make the team, right?"

"I wouldn't say that either," said the coach. "You were quick on your feet. You used good judgement and got out of a tight spot. You get here on time tomorrow, and I'll give you another chance to try out for the team."

"Shortcuts" Discussion Questions

■ Why are taking shortcuts off limits and a particularly bad idea to do by yourself?

■ How did Paul feel about cutting through the vacant lot alone? Why did he do it then?

■ Do you think that Paul would take that chance again? Why or why not?

■ What if the guy who acted like he was supposed to go with him had a badge or a uniform? If you were in Paul's place what would you do then?

■ Was there anything else Paul should have done besides running away to be safe?

■ When would it be OK to go with a policeman or security guard?

Reinforce

■ Kids are most at risk for being kidnapped when they are out alone. It's always safer to go places with a friend rather than alone. An isolated place is also very unsafe because there are no people around to help if you need it.

■ "Trust your feelings. If your feelings are telling you that something doesn't feel right then don't do it.

■ It is dangerous when an adult acts like they are a guard or police just to get kids to go with them. This is a trick used by dangerous people who hurt kids. Never let yourself be alone with a person who acts this way and make sure you go or stay where there are lots of people such as the nearest store and get help from someone you are sure works there.

■ It is important to call 911 immediately and report that someone scared or threatened you. This can help another child from being hurt and you can feel safer too, knowing that the police are checking it out.

Activity 4 — What Kids Need to Know to Stay Away from Danger

Explain

Although most people are good people and safe to be around, it helps a kid be safe and stay away from danger if you know what kinds of people are not safe to be alone with and what dangerous situations to watch out for.

Cover the following information with the whole class. Someone is not a "safe person" to be alone with when that person is:

- **a stranger** — it is never safe to be alone with someone you do not know or know well, even if they seem nice and look OK. If you are by yourself in public, even if you are surrounded by lots of people, and a stranger tries to be friendly and have a conversation with you, it is not a safe thing to do. Strangers who may be dangerous often try to become a child's friend before trying to get a child to go somewhere alone with them.

- **anyone who touches you in a way that makes you feel uncomfortable** — get away from that person as fast as you can whether he or she is a stranger or someone you know well.

- **anyone who tries to trick you into going somewhere alone with them by saying "follow me," "come with me," or "get in the car"** — these are tricks used by dangerous people. Never trust someone who tries to trick you into going with them.

- **anyone who says, "Its OK not to follow your parents' rules. It will be our secret"** — anytime someone asks you to keep a secret or to promise not to tell your parents about something that happened or something they want you to do, then something is wrong. Adults who are safe to be around will say instead, "I understand you have rules about opening the door, accepting a ride, or going with someone. I will wait for you to get permission first."

- **anyone your parents have not given you permission to go with or be alone with who says its OK to go with them anyway** — this is a very unsafe person to go anywhere with. Adults who are safe to be around will say instead, "You are right to ask first. That's the safe thing to do."

- **anyone who makes you feel "Uh-oh. This doesn't feel right"** — anytime someone makes you feel uncomfortable that is a person who is not safe for you to be alone with.

What-if Situations:

Explain that now we are going to learn about dangerous situations to watch out for to help you be safe and stay away from danger.

166

Break the class up into five working groups and give each group a different what-if situation to work with from the Stay-Away-from-Danger What-If Situations page found in this section.

Give each student in the group a copy of Stay-Away-from-Danger Safety Checklist (Handout #1). Explain they will need to refer to this checklist when answering the discussions questions.

Instruct each group of students to process the discussion questions based on the situation provided. One or two students should note the responses.

Ask the groups to then take turns presenting to the class as a whole their what-if situation and answers to the discussion questions.

Then have volunteers from each group act out the safe thing to do and say to stay away from danger for each situation incorporating items from the What to Always Do safety checklist.

Stay-Away-from-Danger What-If Situations

Situation #1

Billy is playing ball with some friends at a neighborhood playground. The ball rolls out of bounds toward the street and he runs to get it. Just then a car pulls up not far from where the ball landed. The man in the car calls to him. He leans over and opens the front car door. He has a map on the front seat. He says, "I'm lost and I need to get to the hospital right away. My child is there and is very sick. I need to get to her. Could you come over here please and show me on the map where we are now so I could find it?" Billy agrees to take a look at the map on the front seat of the car.

Discuss

- Why is this not a safe person to be alone with?
- What tricks does the man use to get the boy to come close to the car?
- What could happen if Billy gets too close to the stranger in the car?
- Refer to the never-to-do safety checklist (Handout #1). Discuss which examples could help you stay away from danger in a similar situation?
- Refer to the always-to-do safety checklist (Handout #1). Decide which ones apply. Have members of the group demonstrate for the class the safe thing to do and say to stay away from danger in a similar situation.

Situation #2

Adam was at the video arcade in town. He was about to beat his personal best when he ran out of money. He asked his friend to lend him some but his friend didn't have any either. A man overheard him and said, "Hey aren't you Adam? I thought I recognized you. Don't you know who I am? I work in the pizza store across from your school."

Adam recognized him and said, "Sure, I know you. We sometimes talk about the baseball scores. Sure, I do."

The man then said, "I was watching you play and you are really good. I am trying to learn the game myself and would love to watch you some more but I have to get going to work. I'll lend you the money. You can just pay me back by showing me how to play next time I see you. Deal? Come with me the change is in the car."

Since Adam knew this guy, he thought it would be OK to borrow some change from him. After all he knew where he worked and could pay him back. He followed him to the car.

Discuss:

■   Why is this not a safe person to be alone with?

■   What tricks does the man use to get Adam to follow him out of the store alone?

■   Refer to the never-to-do safety checklist (Handout #1). Discuss which examples could help you stay away from danger in a similar situation?

■   Refer to the always-to-do safety checklist (Handout #1). Decide which ones apply. Have members of the group demonstrate for the class the safe thing to do and say to stay away from danger in a similar situation.

Situation #3

Suzie is at the flea market with her mom and a friend Bonnie. Her mom said it would be OK for them to stay at the booth that sells really cool jewelry while her mom picks up the book she ordered on the next isle. Suzie suddenly remembered that she left her package at the last booth they were at. She asked Bonnie to come with her but Bonnie said she wasn't finished looking at the jewelry. Suzie said she would go herself and would meet Bonnie and her mother back at the jewelry booth in a few minutes. When Susie was walking alone, all of a sudden a stranger came over and grabbed her arm and started to pull her in the opposite direction, away from Bonnie and her mom. Suzie start to screech and yell, "I don't want to go with you. I don't want to go with you." There are lots people around but no one stopped to help her.

Discuss:

■   Why is this not a safe person to be alone with?

■   When Suzie screeched why didn't people around her stop to help her?

■   Refer to the Never-To-Do safety checklist (Handout #1). Discuss which examples could help you stay away from danger in a similar situation?

■   Refer to the Always-To-Do safety checklist (Handout #1). Decide which ones apply. Have members of the group demonstrate for the class the safe thing to do and say to stay away from danger in a similar situation.

Situation #4

Jimmy is walking home from school alone. He usually walks with his best friend but Dan is home sick. A man he doesn't know pulls up in a white van. He gets out and says, "Jimmy, I am so glad I found you. Your mom said you'd be wearing your T-shirt with your name on it. Your mom is sick and in the hospital. I am supposed to take you to her. Hurry up and get in the car." Jimmy got very worried and started towards the car.

Discuss

■ Why is this not a safe person to be alone with?

■ What tricks does the man use to try and get Jimmy to get in the car and go with him?

■ What if the man was someone he recognized from the neighborhood but he didn't know him well would it be safe for Jimmy to go with him?

■ Refer to the never-to-do safety checklist (Handout #1). Discuss which examples could help you stay away from danger in a similar situation?

■ Refer to the always-to-do safety checklist (Handout #1). Decide which ones apply. Have members of the group demonstrate for the class the safe thing to do and say to stay away from danger in a similar situation.

Situation #5

Sara was lost. One minute she was with her dad in the store looking at CD players and the next minute her dad was nowhere to be seen. She started to look all over the stereo department where she last saw her dad. Then she wandered around the store to see where he could have gone and yelled for her dad. Just then a man came up to her and said, "You look lost. I will help you. I saw a man looking for his daughter in the parking lot. I work in this store. Come with me." Sara followed the man out the store.

Discuss

■ Why is this not a safe person to be alone with?

■ What tricks does the man use to get Sara to follow him out of the store alone?

■ Refer to the never-to-do safety checklist (Handout #1). Discuss which examples could help you stay away from danger in a similar situation?

■ Refer to the always-to-do safety checklist (Handout #1). Decide which ones apply. Have members of the group demonstrate for the class the safe thing to do and say to stay away from danger in a similar situation.

Handout #1
Stay Away from Danger Safety Checklist

What Kids Should Always Do to Stay Away from Danger

☐ Ask permission before getting in a car with anyone.

☐ Ask permission before going anywhere with anyone, even if its someplace or someone you have gone with before.

☐ Ask permission before you take anything from anyone.

☐ Ask permission before opening the door if you are alone or not.

☐ Stay far away from a stranger in a car who asks for help or directions. Tell them to ask another adult for help.

☐ Run in the opposite direction of a car when someone in the car tries to get you to go somewhere with them.

☐ Run away from danger and toward people or into the nearest store and ask for help from a person who works in the store or behind the counter.

☐ If someone tries to touch you, or force you to go with them, yell as loudly as you can, "Help me. This is not my mother/father," or "This person is trying to touch me or kidnap me. Help help!"

☐ Go with a friend and stay with your friend(s) when away from home and out in public.

☐ Get away as fast as you can when someone tries to trick you into going with them. Watch out for these tricks: offering money or presents, asking for help with directions or finding a lost pet, a stranger who says get in the car your parent is hurt and I was told to pick you up, being told to follow a security guard somewhere if you are lost.

☐ If you are lost, stay where you last remember seeing your parent(s).

☐ Take the same safe familiar route when going places alone or with your friends.

☐ Tell a grownup about a dangerous person or situation.

☐ Always ask for the code word if someone says they are supposed to pick you up whether you know the person or not.

What Kids Should Never Do to Stay Away from Danger

☐ Never get in a car with someone you don't know or know well.

☐ Never accept a ride with someone you know if you don't have permission first.

☐ Never agree to help an adult. Adults should ask other adults for help.

☐ Never go near a car that stops for directions or help.

- ☐ Never go anywhere alone with someone you don't know or know well.
- ☐ Never go anywhere with someone you don't know well without permission first.
- ☐ Never take money, presents, or anything, even if its something of yours from someone you don't know or know well.
- ☐ Never give your name, address, or phone number to someone you don't know or don't know well when you meet them in person, on the phone, or on the internet.
- ☐ Never open the door for a stranger or someone you don't know well without permission first.
- ☐ Never tell anyone you are home alone.
- ☐ Never openly display your name on clothing, backpacks, or bookbags.
- ☐ Never take short cuts or go to isolated places especially when you are alone.
- ☐ Never go places alone if you can help it.
- ☐ Never agree to meet someone you have chatted with on the internet unless you have permission and an adult goes with you.

Activity 5 — Playing It Safe When Home Alone

Explain

An important part of being safe for older kids is knowing how to be safe when you are home alone. You will learn the safe thing to do before you enter an empty house, how to answer the door and phone safely, and how to handle an emergency.

We are going to practice different situations that can come up if you are home alone. Then you will be asked to make a home alone safety plan with your parents for homework. An important part of that safety plan is discussing with your parents who you should contact if you can not reach one of them and you need help.

Entering an Empty House Safely. Review with the students the safest way to enter an empty house when you are going to be home alone:

- The best place to keep your house key is on a string around your neck or on a chain attached to a belt loop out of sight.
- Don't let anyone else borrow your key.
- Don't hide a spare key in an obvious place because burglars know all about those places.
- Leave a spare key with a friend, neighbor, or your contact person in case you loose your key.
- Whenever you come home, if a window or door is open or something is strange, don't go in. Go instead to a safe neighbor or to a phone and call the police.
- After entering your house, lock the door behind you.
- Call your mom or dad and let them know you arrived home safely.

Answering the door and phone safely when home alone

- Now we are going to practice the safe thing to do when answering the door and phone. You will learn the tricks unsafe people use to try and get someone to open the door.
- For each situation ask the class for two student volunteers to act out a situation in front of the class. Make two sets of index cards. One card will tell the person who is trying to get in what to say. The other card will tell the child who is home alone how to safety respond and what to do.

172

Home-Alone What-If Situations

Person knocks on the door and says:	Child answers the door and says:	Teacher's Response:
"My car broke down. Please let me use the phone."	"I am sorry you will have to use the phone down the street. I have to help my mom now."	Politely saying no is the safest thing to do without revealing that you are home alone.
"I am here to fix the water heater. Your mom told me to come over. Let me in."	"You have to wait while I check with my mom."	Don't say you are home alone just that you have to check first. Then call your mom, dad, or your contact person if necessary. Call the police if the person is trying to trick you.
"Your mom's been in an accident. Let me in so I can take you to her."	"I can't go anywhere with someone if they don't know the code word. What is the code word?"	Call your mom at work to find out if she's OK. If she's not there call your dad first, then your contact person or the police.
"She didn't have a chance to tell me the code word."	"I will go check with my dad."	
"It's the delivery man. I have a present for your mom. You have to open the door and sign for it."	"Mom can't come to the door right now. Please leave the package at the door."	Don't open the door. Don't say you are alone. Call an adult and tell them what happened.
"If you don't sign for it I can't leave it and it's big and special. Open up."	"You will have to come back later then."	

Answering the phone safely

- If someone calls and says let me speak to your mom or dad. Just say my mom or dad can't come to the phone right now. Would you like to leave a message? If they keep asking just repeat your statement. If they still don't take no for an answer tell them I have to go now. Goodbye.

- Do not tell someone on the phone that you are alone. Never tell anyone your name, address, or phone number over the phone. Don't answer any questions about yourself or any other family members on the phone.

- If someone says something to you over the phone that makes you feel uncomfortable hang up and call your parents immediately. If you can't reach a parent call your contact person or if you feel you are in danger call the police.

Review Street Smarts on the Internet (Handout #3) in class

Instruct students that their homework will be to make a home alone safety plan with their parents. Send students home with following handouts for this purpose:

- Home Alone/Safety Plan

- What Kids Should Always Do to Stay Away from Danger
- What Kids Should Never Do to Stay Away from Danger
- Street Smarts on the Internet

Handout #2
Street Smarts on the Internet
Safety Checklist

☐ Another important part of being safe at home is knowing the safe thing to do when you go online. The people you meet online in chat rooms are really strangers that you do not really know. You need to follow the same safety rules that you learned when you are away from home and home alone.

☐ You already know never to give out personal information to someone you don't know or know well when you are away from home and on the phone. The same thing goes for the internet. Never give your name, address, phone number, any personal information, or any pictures of yourself to anyone on the internet.

☐ Anytime someone writes something to a child that is sexual in nature, about how they look, how you look, what they like to do sexually, or send sexual or nude pictures, this person is dangerous and you should tell your parents and get off line and report it to the authorities. These are the kind of people known to abduct and hurt children they meet online.

☐ Also don't respond to or stay online with anyone who says or does something that makes you feel uncomfortable or funny and tell your parents right away.

☐ Set up safety rules with your parents for going online. This means deciding on when, and how long its OK to stay online, and which areas are safe to visit.

☐ You already know never to go anywhere with someone you do not know or know well. You also know never to go with someone without permission first. These safety rules are important to follow with anyone you meet or chat with on the internet. Some kids have been abducted this way. Never agree to get together with someone you meet on the internet without your parents permission and only go if an adult goes with you.

Handout #3
Home-Alone Safety Plan

Dear Parent(s),

Your child is participating in an abduction prevention program to learn child-safety protection skills. This program teaches children never to go anywhere with anyone, get in a car with anyone, open the door for anyone, or give out personal information in person or on the phone to anyone without a parent's permission first. It is important to make a safety plane if your child stays home alone. The following is a safety checklist to review with your child to make sure your child knows what to do to be safe if home alone and when away from home.

Discuss with your child

1) Where your child should safely keep the house key (if they carry one)?

2) Who will keep a spare key?

3) Who should your child go to for help if he or she goes home to an empty house and things don't look right?

4) Who should your child contact (at least two names) in case your child needs help and can't reach a parent?

5) Who does your child have permission to open the door for when home alone?

6) Make up a secret code word with your child. Your child should never go anywhere with anyone unless they have permission to go with that person. If you send someone to pick up your child and they know the secret code word, then it is safe to go. If someone tries to get your child to go with them or open the door and the person does not know the secret code word then your child will know not to listen to that person.

7) It is safest for your child to put the computer in the family room so that you can monitor its use. If your child goes online set up online safety rules with your child:

   - What time of day is it OK for your child to go online? (Keep in mind that most child pornography is transferred after 11 p.m.)

   - How long is it OK to stay online?

   - What are the safe areas your child is allowed to visit online? (It's safest to visit are kids' chat rooms and kids' sites.)

6) Post a list of emergency and important phone numbers by the phone. Include the following numbers:

   - Home address and phone number

   - Mom's work number

   - Dad's work number

- Doctor's number
- Names and number of two contact people
- Police and fire department, 911

Review with your child what to do when calling 911. Make sure your child knows that he or she should give their name, address, phone number, and reason for the call. Instruct your child not to hang up until the operator tells them it is OK.

7) The following safety checklists are being sent home for you to review with your child. This will give you an overview of what your child learned in school about abduction prevention. By going over this material with your child you will be reinforcing important child protection rules to help keep your child safe.

- What Kids Should Always Do to Stay Away From Danger
- What Kids Should Never Do to Stay Away From Danger
- Street Smarts On the Internet